MINDFULNESS ON THE RUN

Dr Chantal Hofstee is a clinical psychologist who works in both private and corporate sectors. She combines Cognitive Behavioural Therapy techniques with research-based mindfulness training to equip her clients with easy-to-use skills that transform their lives. Through her company **Renew Your Mind**, she and her team provide mindfulness courses and business training to enable people to take control of stress, improve focus, solve problems and become more innovative. Find out more about Chantal at: **www.mindfulnessontherun.com**

MINDFULNESS ON THE RUN

QUICK, EFFECTIVE MINDFULNESS TECHNIQUES FOR BUSY PEOPLE

DR CHANTAL HOFSTEE

EXISLE
PUBLISHING

First published 2016

Exisle Publishing Pty Ltd
'Moonrising', Narone Creek Road, Wollombi, NSW 2325, Australia
P.O. Box 60–490, Titirangi, Auckland 0642, New Zealand
www.exislepublishing.com

A CiP record for this book is available from the National Library of Australia.

ISBN 978-1-925335-03-3

Cover design by Enni Tuomisalo
Design and typesetting by Nick Turzynski of redinc. book design
Illustrations by Jessie Miller
Cover photograph of the author by Jasper Boer
Typeset in Alright 11/16
Printed in China

This book uses paper sourced under ISO 14001 guidelines from well-managed forests and other controlled sources.

10 9 8 7 6 5 4 3 2 1

Note
The author would like to acknowledge the work of Jan Bernard, Pauline Skeates and Byron Katie.

Disclaimer

To Pieter,
Thank you.

Contents

Introduction:
MINDFULNESS FOR BUSY PEOPLE

When was the last time you were not busy? How often do you feel stressed? Imagine that you could navigate your most challenging times with a mind that was calm and focused and filled with positive thoughts — what would be different?

Would you feel better? Stay calm when things don't go according to plan? Be more effective at work? Would your relationships be different? Would you be kinder to yourself?

It's easy to see stress as a normal part of life. But it does not have to be that way. I used to feel tired and stressed most of the time. My life felt like a never-ending race to do more, do better and tick the boxes on my to-do list, only to then add new things to it. Negative chatter and worries crowded my thoughts and I needed to achieve more and more to feel good about myself. All of this made it hard to be present and enjoy life.

I am grateful that those days are gone, and I have mindfulness practice to thank for it.

Mindfulness is very effective in reducing stress, and it doesn't have to be difficult or time-consuming; you don't have to go away on a retreat or sit still for 20 minutes a day to calm your busy mind. Mindfulness can be simple and practical. In this book I will show how you can practice mindfulness *on the run* by fitting it into your everyday activities so you can enjoy a busy life without a busy mind.

Research shows that mindfulness effectively:

Reduces	Increases
Stress	Physical health
Anxiety	Emotion regulation
Depression	Productivity
Impulsivity	Overall wellbeing and happiness

These techniques changed me from a stressed and anxious over-committer to a content and mindful partner, parent and entrepreneur — and they could do the same for you.

This book will:

- Give you insights into the functioning of your brain.
- Help you understand the origins of your unhelpful patterns that cause stress.
- Teach you practical mindfulness techniques that you can use in the midst of busy days.

Each chapter has a section called 'Insight inspiration'. It contains questions that are designed to help you relate the theory to your personal life. This creates powerful insights, which increase the effectiveness of the mindfulness exercises. You might want to use a notebook or journal to write down your answers to the questions in this section.

To reach results more quickly and easily, I recommend the 'Mindfulness on the Run' CD or download. It has recordings of the mindfulness exercises you'll find in this book. This way you don't have to remember the steps, you just turn on the track of the technique you want to practise and hear my voice guiding you through the steps. Your practice couldn't be easier.

You can purchase the CD or download it from our website: **www.mindfulnessontherun.com**

Today I am a clinical psychologist. But I first discovered mindfulness practice years ago, when I was a student, and it became a very effective stress-reduction tool through my university days. Years later, however, I found myself highly stressed, trying to juggle my roles as a partner, a parent and a principal in a busy psychology practice. I just couldn't find the time to keep up my mindfulness practice, which led to a dilemma:

> *You need mindfulness practice the most when you are busy and stressed, but during those times you cannot go on a retreat or set aside 20 minutes a day to meditate — you are simply too busy!*

My life was not going to change any time soon, so I had two options: either give up practising mindfulness, or create a way of practising mindfulness that would fit in with my busy lifestyle. This led me to develop the 'Renew Your Mind' method: mindfulness techniques that are practical and highly effective, yet do not require you to sit still and meditate but instead can be done 'on the run'.

Let me share a real-life example of how I use mindfulness on the run to combat stress. Just recently I was packing my things in the morning, and I had exactly 20 minutes before I had to leave the house. I was going to drop off my two-year-old son at his nanny's house and then calmly and mindfully make my way to the university where I was invited to teach mindfulness to a group of 32 students.

At the time our house was being renovated, so we were staying with friends. As I was preparing for the day my son was watching a *Thomas the Tank Engine* DVD in my friend's beautiful home office. When all my things were packed, I went to get him — and found him drawing on her expensive, white office chair with a black marker. He could see the horror on my face and in an attempt to make me feel better he pointed at the drawing and said, 'Mama, Thomas the train!' I took a deep breath and suppressed the urge to scream '*NO!!!!!!*' I calmly took the pen away from him and said, 'Drawings on paper not on chairs, please.'

I tried to clean the chair with soap and water but the thick black stripes wouldn't come off. Then I remembered I had read that milk can help remove pen from fabrics, so I poured a tiny bit of milk on a cloth and tried to clean the chair, but with no result. So, I went to the kitchen again to try the soap one more time. At this point I was already five minutes late.

When I ran back into the office, I discovered that my son had emptied the entire bottle of milk on the white, fabric chair! Half of the milk was on the chair and the other half had ended up on the beige, woollen carpet. Before I knew it a loud '*No!*' came from my mouth, which resulted in him crying as I rushed to the kitchen to get towels.

At this point I was 10 minutes late, had a crying child and a bottle of milk spilled on an expensive chair and carpet in my friend's home office. And there it was — the adrenaline and cortisol were kicking my stress response into gear. I could feel my breathing changing, my heart rate increasing and tunnel vision kicking in. Realizing that going into stress mode was not going to help me, I used mindfulness to calm myself down. I focused on my breathing and calmed myself so I could make a plan. I called the nanny and asked her to come over and pick up my son. Then I comforted my son while trying to clean up the mess. When the nanny arrived I was 20 minutes late but I'd done the best I could to clean the mess. I jumped in the car and put the university address into my GPS system.

Then the thoughts came . . . *What have I done? The milk is going to smell so bad. It will leave a big stain. My friend is going to be so upset!* Knowing that there is absolutely no point, or benefit, to stressing out, I calmed my brain down with mindfulness of the senses: looking at the views, listening to the sounds and feeling the steering wheel, the pedals, the seat.

Feeling relatively calm again — knowing that I could still make it to the lecture on time — I noticed that the GPS had directed me somewhere unfamiliar. I stopped the car to check the address. Yes, I had put in the right address . . .

Ten minutes later I found myself in a part of town that was definitely not right. With just five minutes until the lecture was due to start I called the college to confirm the location and discovered I was 20 minutes away from it! Despair, frustration and pointless anger towards my phone kicked in. Again, I realized that this would not help me, it would only make me drive around like a mad woman, which isn't good for anyone. So, I used the beginner's mind technique to calm myself down again. I focused on the facts: *I am in the car, driving to the college. The GPS brought me to the wrong place, but I know where I am going now and the students will be informed I am on my way.* This worked for a little while, until different thoughts started to creep in: *They are all going to think I am useless and that I don't care about being on time. They will never ever invite me back. No one will listen to my lecture. How can they take me seriously when I can't even manage to show up on time? And by the way, I have ruined my friend's carpet!*

My inner critic always picks excellent moments to show up! But I knew I could tackle it with the self-inquiry technique. After working through each of my negative thoughts, asking myself if I actually knew each was 100 per cent true, I came to realize that none of them was. While my situation was not ideal, it was not the disaster my inner critic had tried to convince me it was.

When I finally arrived, I was calm again; to keep calm I was mindful of my posture, facial expressions and my breathing. The class was happy to see me, and I started my lecture with a story of stress.

'Just image that you are getting ready to deliver a lecture for a group of 32 students and your son is watching a *Thomas the Tank Engine* DVD while you are getting ready . . .'

This example shows that no matter how much mindfulness practice you do, you cannot eradicate stressful and challenging situations from your life; there is no escaping them. Mindfulness is a way to train your brain to become better able to cope with these situations. It gives you a buffer that prevents your stressful thoughts or negative emotions from hijacking your brain and taking control.

This is mindfulness on the run.

Chapter 1:
UNDERSTANDING YOUR BRAIN

When you want to make changes to the way you think and feel, it is important to understand the very thing that is making you think and feel: your brain. Your brain is your most important asset, a power station that connects your every thought, feeling and action. Without your brain, there is no you. Yet people tend to take better care of their teeth, their hair and even their car than their brain. Understanding how your brain works helps you to take care of it and make it work better.

Your brain is made up mostly of water, about 10 per cent fats and 100,000 miles of blood vessels. The brain's basic building blocks are called neurons, and your brain has around 100 billion of them, each with between 1000 and 10,000 connections with other neurons. Information is passed along these connections through chemical messages and electrical impulses. These connections are called neural pathways and I will also refer to them as pathways or roads within the brain.

Neuroplasticity

Scientists used to think that the brain is fixed and hardwired by the time we become an adult. Research in only the past decade tells us that this is simply not true. The brain is flexible and changes throughout our lives, and this process is called neuroplasticity.

You can think of your brain as a dynamic power station, with many neural pathways that light up each time you think, feel or do something. The more a pathway is used, the thicker and stronger it becomes. This makes it easy for your brain to travel that road. If you make a conscious effort to think, feel or do something differently, your brain begins to carve out a new road, which means a new pathway is established.

Brain training

Your brain is constantly changing and adapting based on your experiences. Changing old habits and creating new ones comes with directed and repeated practice of the new way of thinking, feeling and doing. By practising the mindfulness techniques described in this book, you will literally rewire your brain. The techniques function as a circuit breaker that stops old, unhelpful patterns from being reinforced. They allow you to introduce and build new, more helpful roads. By doing this over and over again, the new pathways will become strong and take over. Eventually this new way of thinking, feeling or doing becomes second nature.

This process is not very different from physical exercise. Let's take push-ups as an example. Every single time you do a push-up you are changing something in the structure of your muscles. The more you practise, the stronger the muscles and easier the exercise becomes.

It takes six to eight weeks of daily practice for a new way of thinking, feeling or doing to form a strong new neural pathway. The good news is that even if you don't practise on a daily basis, you will start to notice changes within just a few weeks. The only requirement is that you do the exercises regularly.

The learning process has the following four phases.

Phase	Category	Old pathway	New pathway
1	unaware unskilled	existing	not existing
2	consciously unskilled	dominant	existing
3	consciously skilled	existing	dominant
4	unaware skilled	not existing	existing

PHASE 1: UNAWARE UNSKILLED

When you decide to start practising mindfulness you are motivated to make changes. For most people at this stage, the desire to feel different is what drives them. When it comes to skills, at this stage you are unaware unskilled because you haven't yet been introduced to the mindfulness skills. Your old pathways and habits are strong and no new pathways have been built — yet.

PHASE 2: CONSCIOUSLY UNSKILLED

In the early days of your mindfulness practice, your brain begins to form new pathways. It requires effort and conscious attention for your brain to build and use these new pathways because the old pathways are still dominant and therefore easier to use. In this phase it can be a real challenge to keep practising!

PHASE 3: CONSCIOUSLY SKILLED

After some weeks of doing the exercises you will notice that your practice becomes a lot easier. New pathways have been established and are strengthening. At some point the new pathways will become the dominant ones. But be aware — in times of stress, the old pathways can still take over quite quickly!

PHASE 4: UNAWARE SKILLED

In the last phase of retraining your brain, the old pathways have become dormant or have disappeared. New pathways have become 'roads well travelled'. Your practice is still important to keep the roads maintained, but you will notice you are practising mindfulness without conscious effort. You have become a more mindful person. At this point, a mindful way of thinking, feeling and doing has become second nature.

The green brain and the red brain

The way your perceptions, thoughts and emotions work and interact is quite complex. They are constantly changing and consist of many different layers. Some are part of your conscious mind, while others are part of your subconscious mind. At any given moment, when you peel away the different layers of thoughts and emotions all the way to the bottom of your subconscious mind, there are two options: your brain either feels safe or unsafe. Throughout this book I will refer to the unsafe state as the red-brain state and the safe state as the green-brain state. All of your thoughts, feelings and actions in that moment will come from either the safe (green) or unsafe (red) brain state.

There are various levels of safe or unsafe — you can picture this as a spectrum: at one end is the extremely safe green brain, and at the other end is the extremely unsafe red brain. Where your brain is on the spectrum depends on the situation, as well as your current thoughts.

GREEN
BRAIN

RED
BRAIN

THE RED BRAIN

The red-brain state is a state of stress. You can see the state of stress as a fire alarm. Stress is activated when the mind perceives a threat, this activates the fight-or-flight response, which is actually very useful when there is a physical threat. It is, after all, what keeps you alive when you are faced with danger. When the fight-or-flight response kicks in, your brain and body are in the best possible state to deal with a threat, hence ensuring the greatest chance of survival.

The red brain can be triggered when there is no actual physical threat. Your brain reacts to how safe or unsafe you *perceive* a situation to be. Therefore, your thoughts are the most important factor in determining how your brain assesses a situation. For example, if you fear public speaking and say to yourself, 'I can't do this' or, 'This will be a disaster', your brain perceives the situation as unsafe and the stress response is activated. In this state the hormones cortisol and adrenaline are released, creating the following effects.

Physical effects:
- Tunnel vision
- Shallow breathing
- Stopped or slowed digestion
- Increased blood pressure and blood sugar
- Increased heart rate
- Suppressed immune system
- Tensed muscles

Psychological effects:
- Judgmental and black-and-white thinking
- Feeling stressed
- Narrow or fixed point of view
- Unkind manner
- Disconnection from others

The consequences of these effects include:
- Overlooking information
- Referring back to old patterns
- Bad decision-making and prioritizing
- Approaching problems with familiar solutions
- Miscommunications
- Decreased compassion and empathy

Having the fight-or-flight option available is essential for you to be able to deal with extreme situations — such as being attacked by a snake, running from a fire or seeing a child run onto the road. When you are running from a fire you need tunnel vision, tensed muscles, increased heart rate and blood pressure because these things help you to move as quickly as you can. On the other hand, being kind and considerate is not a priority — you simply don't have time to think about how your grandmother is doing when you are running for your life! It is all about survival, and unnecessary functions, including your immune system and digestive system, are put on hold.

The state of stress is not helpful at all when you are worrying about a deadline, a messy house or a difficult conversation. Because of all the symptoms listed above, the red brain makes it more difficult for you to deal with non-threatening situations in a good way.

Another reason the red brain should be reserved for emergency situations only is that spending too much time in the state of stress damages both your brain and your body. It is designed to get you safely through extreme circumstances and then return to a state of calm. Once the snake has left, your system can calm down again. When the fire is put out the system can relax. The problem with stress caused by non-threatening situations is that there is often no calming down. When you are in the state of stress too often or stay there for too long you risk ongoing negative physical consequences such as high blood pressure and heart failure and psychological problems such as burnout, anxiety, depression and post-traumatic stress disorder.

If you want to live a healthy and balanced life, the red-brain state does not have to be eliminated but should be reserved for emergency situations only.

THE GREEN BRAIN

The green-brain state, or as I like to call it 'calm and present', is on the opposite end of the spectrum. In this brain state the stress hormones cortisol and adrenaline are reduced and the 'relationship hormone' oxytocin is released, stimulating the following responses.

Physical effects:
- Wide vision and flexible attention
- Deep breathing
- Optimal digestion
- Reduced blood pressure and blood sugar
- Reduced heart rate
- Optimal immune system
- Relaxed muscles

Psychological effects:
- Non-judgmental thinking
- Feeling calm and in control
- Seeing the bigger picture
- Being kind
- Connecting with others

The consequences of these effects include:
- Eye for detail as well as the bigger picture
- Good decision-making and prioritizing
- Creative problem-solving
- Social connection
- More effective communication
- Increased compassion and empathy

Spending time in the green-brain state is essential for your physical health because it is in this state that your breathing, heart rate and blood pressure are able to find their natural base-rate levels. Essentially, your digestive system and immune system work at their best in this state.

In the green-brain state, defenses come down and all the resources in your brain become available to you. Creativity and flexibility are unlocked and you are able to see the bigger picture. It is in this brain state that you can make good decisions and be truly effective and productive. In this state you will also be able to relax and process events and emotions. On top of that, the release of oxytocin immediately increases compassion, empathy and the desire to connect with others. This hormone is the fuel for our relationships and is essential for wellbeing.

THE ORANGE BRAIN

The neutral, middle ground on the spectrum is the state of achieving, which I will refer to as the orange brain. This brain state is the 'go-go-go state', in which you plan and think about goals, and then set about working to achieve them. These goals can be big, such as building a house, or they can be small, such as simply posting a letter. This brain state is an area that falls between the green zone and the red zone on the spectrum. In this state you are telling your brain it will make it to the green zone once this or that task is completed. The orange brain does not have the negative symptoms of the red brain, nor does it have the benefits of the green brain. Because it is so goal-orientated, you can easily move from the orange to the red zone when something prevents you from reaching your goal.

GREEN
BRAIN

ORANGE
BRAIN

RED
BRAIN

It is important to keep in mind that these states fall on a spectrum, and we can move very quickly from one zone to another — sometimes within a split second! Also, there is nothing wrong with any of the brain states. Red, orange and green all serve their own purpose, and there is a time and place for each. Understanding how they affect your health, feelings and behaviour can be very useful because it helps make sense of how you live your life. The goal of mindfulness is not to block any of these states; it is to allow you to take greater control of the state your brain is in.

Productivity myth

Many people spend most of their time going back and forth between the state of achieving (orange brain) and the state of stress (red brain). Being aware and present (green brain) is reserved for special occasions like holidays and is often associated with being lazy and unproductive.

This pattern makes sense because there is a small sub-state that is highly addictive and it is called success. When you reach your goal, the chemicals dopamine and serotonin are released, making you feel great. The sub-state of success can make it easy to get hooked into the pattern: achieving–stress–success. The problem with this pattern is that your happiness becomes tied to reaching your goals, instead of happiness coming from life in general. When your happiness is restricted in this way, it is fleeting and before you know it you are back in the stress or achieving state in order to reach your next goal. This is an unsustainable pattern and ultimately leads to burnout, because we simply cannot function well without having enough green-brain time.

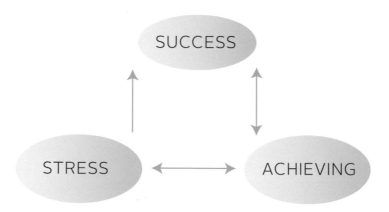

Research tells us that the belief held by many in this busy, modern world that stress increases productivity is simply not true. When you operate from a state of stress you are cognitively slower, make more mistakes, you overlook details and you are less likely to perform well. You might *feel* as if you are doing well, but if you look at it objectively your performance is likely to be poorer than it would be if you were in the calm and present state. In a state of stress you might work harder, but in a state of calm you work smarter.

Working from a state of stress is like driving your car with the handbrake on: you might get from A to B, but it takes a lot of effort and in the long run it does damage.

Spending time in the green-brain state is not a luxury; it is the key to achieving optimal brain activity. Being in this brain state is incredibly healthy — reduced blood pressure and blood sugar, reduced heart rate, optimal digestion and immune system — and allows your body the opportunity to restore itself. Research shows that the green brain is also the ideal brain state for you to be effective and productive because you can see the bigger picture and have all your brain resources available to you, thus allowing your brain to function at its best. When you operate from this brain state you are at your most productive, effective, efficient, flexible and creative, so things seem to come more easily, sometimes even effortlessly.

Spending time in the green-brain state is like servicing your brain, taking care of it to make sure everything runs smoothly. It's just like servicing your car regularly because otherwise it might break down.

When you understand how the brain works and what the different brain states can do for you, prioritizing green-brain activity just makes sense.

What controls the brain states?

When there is a real physical threat, your system immediately moves to the red zone. However, there is another powerful trigger that can set off the red, orange or green brain: your thoughts. Your brain uses your thoughts as cues to determine how safe or unsafe a situation is, and based on this assessment it will activate one of the three states. Underneath all the rational thinking, your brain perceives worries and judgments as threats because they communicate to your brain that something is not right, and the brain then moves to the orange or the red zone.

For example, if you worry about your finances, the thought, 'I don't have enough money' could come up. Your brain sees this thought as a signal for a potential threat and the red brain is activated. Your thoughts keep coming back to the perceived lack of money (fixed point of view) and you lose sight of the bigger picture of your financial situation, stopping you from prioritizing or coming up with creative solutions (bad decision-making). On a physical level you might lose your appetite (slowed digestion), your breathing becomes shallow and your heart rate, blood pressure and blood sugar rise. Your brain and body are getting ready for fight-or-flight, even though there is no physical threat to run from. Your worries about money have then activated the red brain, making you much less able to effectively deal with any financial issues you might have.

It is important to realize that these brain states are linked to certain thoughts and brain activity; they are not directly linked to particular situations (except in the case of a physical threat). Following are some examples.

ON YOUR WAY TO WORK

The red brain: You are getting ready to leave the house to go to work. You are rushing and feel frustrated. All you can think of is what you have to get done that day (fixed point of view); you are not present with what you do and because of this you forget to pack important things (overlooking things) and you cannot remember where you put your keys (lose sight of the bigger picture). When you hit the traffic you become angry and annoyed with other road users (decreased compassion and empathy), and when you arrive at work you are feeling grumpy (negative mood).

The orange brain: You are getting ready to leave the house to go to work. You are focused on this goal (tunnel vision), and everything you do is linked to achieving it. You're keeping an eye on the time to make sure you stay on track. You are multitasking and thinking about work-related things in the meantime, telling yourself that you can relax once this workday is over. When you hit the traffic (obstruction to the goal) you become restless and risk ending up in the red-brain zone.

The green brain: You are getting ready to leave the house to go to work. You are present in the moment while eating your breakfast (optimal digestion), getting dressed and packing your things (more efficient). While driving, you might listen to some music and notice things you see outside. When you hit the traffic you accept this and don't let it ruin your mood. You are appreciative of the moment and can fully enjoy it in a relaxed way. You arrive at work in a good mood and are able to concentrate and work efficiently. You feel connected to your colleagues and are able to offer help and support when they need it.

LYING ON THE BEACH WITH A COCKTAIL

The red brain: You are lying on the beach with a cocktail, feeling irritated by the heat, the temperature of the water and even the sand beneath your feet! You might be annoyed with the waiter for getting your order wrong, feeling disappointed with the hotel because it is not quite what you expected and angry because your children are too loud. You are lying on the beach with a cocktail feeling tense, restless and frustrated with what is happening around you.

The orange brain: You are lying on the beach with a cocktail, planning the rest of the day. You are thinking about all the sights you want to see, the activities you want to do and when you want to do them. You're there planning and organizing and lose sight of all that is happening around you.

The green brain: You are lying on the beach with a cocktail, really being present in that moment: feeling the warm sun on your skin, the soft sand under your feet, hearing the sounds and watching your children play. Your breathing is deep, your heart rate is slow, and you are happy in that moment, just as it is.

The red-, orange- or green-brain states are all useful; they are simply designed for different purposes. Red deals with physical threats, green focuses on life in general, and orange is the middle ground. Learning how to be more in control of your thoughts will give you more control over the brain state you are in.

INSIGHT INSPIRATION

1. What brain state are you in most of your time? Red, orange or green?

2. Can you identify how you move between the three brain states?

3. How has this pattern affected your life? (Think health, relationships, work, etc.)

Chapter 2:
INTRODUCING MINDFULNESS

How can you train your brain to spend more time in the green-brain state and be more calm and present, as well as your most productive self? Mindfulness practice is a way of retraining your brain and learning how to 'switch on' this healthy, green-brain state. Before I show you how this works, let me first explain what mindfulness is and what it is not.

What is mindfulness?

Being mindful is a way of being in the world, which involves certain ways of thinking and paying attention. The definition of mindfulness is:

Paying attention with kindness.

Mindfulness has two main components: attention and attitude.

ATTENTION

Most people suffer from what is called a monkey mind. Your mind is like a monkey randomly swinging from branch to branch; your thoughts go from one thing to another, to another, to another. Before you know it you are thinking about something and have no idea how you got there. The monkey mind often thinks about the past, pondering what happened or what you think should have gone differently. Or it thinks about the future, worrying about what might happen or thinking about all the things you have to get done.

If your mind wanders to the past or the future you cannot be present with what is happening right now, which is a problem because the only thing that you *can* influence is the now. You cannot go back in time and change what has already happened, and who knows what the future holds? Your monkey mind is blocking you from being present in — and truly enjoying — the now. When you are not present with what is happening but thinking about other things, you are not able to effectively influence the present. Therefore, mindfulness is about taming the monkey mind and regaining control of your thoughts by focusing on the now.

'An unstable mind is like an unstable camera, you get a fuzzy picture.'
— **CHRISTOPHER GERMER**

This does not mean that you will never look back or plan ahead. Instead you are training your mind to be able to stay in the now. This puts you back in the driver's seat so that you — and not the monkey mind — decide where your thoughts go next.

ATTITUDE

Being kind and non-judgmental is at the core of mindfulness practice. This means that you accept what is, without arguing with the facts or thinking things should be different. This sounds simple, but when you start to practise mindfulness you will realize that you judge things, others and yourself all the time:

- He shouldn't have said that.
- You're wearing the wrong shoes.
- The house looks horrible!
- What a grumpy waiter.
- My back hurts.
- The dog is too loud.
- Why can't I just focus?
- That fence is so ugly.

As soon as you have a judgmental thought you send a signal to your brain that something is not right. This activates the orange or red brain and blocks the green brain. Mindfulness is about taming the inner critic, about erasing the *should*s and the *shouldn't*s from your thinking and accepting everything as it is without arguing with the facts.

Remember, this does not mean that you stop making changes and just let everything be as it is. This is about training yourself to think in a way that reduces unhelpful stress so you can be more effective in reaching your goals. After a kind and non-judgmental thought you can still decide to do something about a situation. Then you will be making changes from the ideal brain state rather than from a state of stress. It allows you to become *responsive* instead of *reactive*.

Here are some examples of judgmental thinking versus mindful thinking.

Judgmental thinking: He left his glass on the bench again! I am so sick of this, how many times do I have to tell him! How difficult can it be?

Mindful thinking: He left his glass on the bench. This is the way it is right now. How do I want to respond?

Judgmental thinking: My back hurts and it is so annoying! Why does this have to happen to me? It is so unfair.
Mindful thinking: I have a strong sensation in my back. This is the way it is right now. What would help?

Judgmental thinking: It is so rude and unprofessional of them to ignore my email. Argggghh, this is so annoying, it shows a complete lack of respect!
Mindful thinking: They are not responding to my email. It is what it is. How do I want to respond to this situation?

What mindfulness is not

There are four common myths about mindfulness.

1. Mindfulness is Buddhism

Mindfulness is often associated with Buddhism. However, mindfulness does not belong to any religion, culture or group. It has been practised by many different people in various cultures and religions and it has been called by many different names including meditation, centring prayer, contemplation or simply paying attention. Practising mindfulness is an inherent human capacity that is available to everyone.

2. Mindfulness is airy-fairy

Research-based mindfulness practice is based on a multitude of scientific studies and understanding of the brain. The number of scientific studies that have been done on mindfulness has increased drastically over the past few years and keeps growing. At the moment, more than 3000 scientific studies have been conducted on the subject, and most of them show positive results. However, not all of these studies have strong validity and a lot of improvements are yet to be made in the field of scientific research on mindfulness. Many of these studies and meta analyses can be viewed via the online database of the American Mindfulness Research Association (www.goamra.org).

3. Mindfulness is for hippies

You don't have to be even slightly alternative to practise mindfulness. In fact, even the corporate world has discovered that mindfulness is a stress-combat hero that increases creativity, innovation and productivity. No wonder businesses such as Apple, Google and Goldman Sachs are making mindfulness training available to their staff.

4. Mindfulness involves yoga

Mindfulness does not involve yoga or any other form of physical exercise. Mindfulness can be used during yoga or physical exercise but they are not the same thing. Mindfulness is about training your brain. There is no need for physical activity or challenging positions.

Self-compassion

When your thoughts become kinder and less judgmental an interesting side effect takes place. The way you relate to yourself changes. You grow in self-compassion and kindness towards yourself. Many people are incredibly harsh on themselves, constantly beating themselves up. This internal dialogue is a huge source of stress, but when you learn to be kind and non-judgmental towards yourself, you are reshaping your inner world and turning it from an unsafe place into a safe place. This promotes green-brain activity instead of red-brain activity. You are doing your mind a huge favour by eradicating what might be the biggest source of stress you will ever have in your life.

When I stopped judging my husband for putting his glass on the bench instead of in the dishwasher, I was better able to address it in a calm and effective way. When I stopped complaining about my back pain I found that it eased. When I didn't judge the lack of response to my email I could deal with it in a calm but assertive manner. You will be better able to reach your goals if you can keep your brain in the green zone or bring it back to a calm and present state *before* you respond. It may feel counter-intuitive, but when you practise present-moment awareness and kind and non-judgmental thoughts, you are increasing the likelihood of successfully making the changes you want to make.

> *Mindfulness is brain manipulation for a good cause.*

The power of mindfulness

As you start to practise mindfulness you are activating the green brain more and more. Everything you practise becomes stronger, so the more you activate the green brain, the stronger the green brain pathways become and the easier it will be for your brain to access this state. This has a huge positive effect on both your physical and mental health.

Research shows that regular mindfulness practice does the following.

Reduces	Increases
Stress	Compassion
Anxiety	Emotion regulation
Depression	Body regulation
Blood pressure	Productivity
Obsessive–compulsive symptoms	Enjoyment of food
Substance abuse	Self-compassion
Post-traumatic stress	General wellbeing
Impulsivity	Creative thinking
Inflammation	
Bipolar disorder symptoms	

Brain hygiene

Every time you do a mindfulness exercise you are taking care of your brain by building and maintaining green-brain pathways. You could call it brain hygiene. You brush your teeth a few times a day to make sure they stay healthy and strong and to prevent problems; practising mindfulness does the same for your brain. Mindfulness exercises give your brain a break, clean it up and make sure it stays healthy.

Mindfulness for improving focus

By focusing on what is happening right in front of you, in this moment, you are practising mindfulness. Focusing on your breath or on your senses is a simple way to bring your attention to the present moment.

You can practise this technique any time and anywhere. You don't have to sit still; you can practise while you are doing your morning stretches, taking a walk or when you are driving to work. It does not matter when or how you do it as long as you do it regularly. For your initial practice I recommend you dedicate a particular moment each day, and it often helps to tie your practice to something you are already doing. This way it is easier to remember to do your exercises and you don't have to reserve extra time for it.

This technique comes easily to some people, yet it is hard for others. If you find your thoughts wandering off a lot, it is absolutely fine! Every single time you bring your attention back to your breath or one of your senses, you are practising mindfulness. In time you will find it easier and your thoughts won't wander off as much. A green-brain state is essential for effective learning and neuroplasticity, therefore it is important to keep a positive and patient attitude. Don't make your practice too hard. If you struggle practising for five minutes, then practise for three minutes, and try to stay kind and non-judgmental in the process.

I begin most days with a mindfulness exercise. I take my fresh cup of coffee out onto my beautiful rooftop deck, and for at least three minutes I focus my attention on the moment. In these three minutes I fully take in my surroundings. I feel the breeze on my skin, I listen to the birds and I notice my breathing. I also fully take in and enjoy my cup of coffee, by smelling it and tasting it with awareness.

These three minutes without distractions such as my phone or laptop help me to clear my head, centre myself and start the day in the green-brain state. To me this is the best possible start to each day.

EXERCISE 1:
MINDFULNESS OF THE BREATH

Step 1. Focus on your breath.

Step 2. Notice what it feels like to breathe in and out. Notice this without giving your opinion, or wanting to change anything. Simply feel the air and notice what happens in your body as you breathe in and out.

Step 3. If your thoughts wander off, notice this. Then, in a kind and gentle way, bring your attention back to your breath.

Tip: You can see your thoughts as butterflies or clouds that come and go. Just let them float past without engaging with them and turn your attention back to your breath.

EXERCISE 2:
MINDFULNESS OF THE SENSES

Step 1. Focus on what you hear.

Step 2. Observe and describe this, either in your mind or out loud. Do this in a kind, neutral and non-judgmental way, without labelling or giving your opinion. Simply describe the sounds that you hear.

For example, *I hear the clock ticking. I hear the birds singing. I hear the dog barking*.

Step 3. Then focus on what you see.

Step 4. Again observe and describe this in a kind, neutral and non-judgmental way without giving your opinion. Simply describe the sights that you see.

For example, *I see my desk. I see a tree. I see the light reflecting on the wall.*

Step 5. Then focus on what you physically feel.

Step 6. Observe and describe this in a kind and non-judgmental way. Simply notice and describe what you physically feel. If you feel any discomfort or tension, try to notice this, without wanting to change it or fix it.

For example, *I feel the floor underneath my feet. I feel a sensation in my lower back* (instead of *I feel pain). I feel my clothing on my skin.*

Step 7. Now focus on what you taste.

Step 8. Observe and describe what you taste in a kind and non-judgmental way, without labelling or giving your opinion. Notice the subtlety of what you taste and where in your mouth you taste it.

For example, *I taste peppermint tea. I taste something sweet on the tip of my tongue. I taste a subtle salty taste on the sides of my tongue.*

Step 9. Focus on what you smell.

Step 10. Observe and describe what you smell without judging or giving your opinion. If you don't smell anything, then just notice that.

For example, *I smell a scented candle. I smell coffee. I smell nothing.*

Tip: You can either do the full exercise, from step 1 through to step 10, or you can choose to focus on only some of your senses. The order in which you do this is irrelevant. I recommend that you try all of them and then keep using the ones you find most calming and centring.

EXERCISE 3:
MINDFUL EATING

Steps 7–10 from Exercise 2 can be used to do a mindfulness exercise called mindful eating. Complete this exercise by eating or drinking something and paying full attention to what you taste and smell. By bringing awareness to what you are eating you increase your experience and you will have greater control over what you eat and how much you eat.

 On-the-run tip: *Put your commute time to good use by spending a few minutes focusing on your senses on your way to work.*

Chapter 3:
MINDFULNESS AND EMOTIONS

Have you ever wondered why some people always seem to have a positive outlook on life regardless of challenges and disappointments? And why others, who seem to have it all, worry and are unsatisfied and judgmental?

Your base-rate happiness is determined by several factors, one of which is your personality. Some people are naturally resilient and have a more positive outlook than others. Another factor is your upbringing. How did your parents handle negative events? What sort of response did they model? It is likely that your way of responding to negative emotions is somewhat similar. Also, your coping mechanisms, the strategies you use to manage internal or external stress, impact how you process negative events and emotions.

There are four basic emotions that humans can experience:

■ Anger

■ Fear

■ Happiness

■ Sadness

All the other emotions that we experience fall under one of these four categories. For example, nervousness falls under fear, irritation falls under anger, and cheerfulness falls under happiness.

All emotions are important and they are there for good reasons. If humans did not experience any fear we would have become extinct a long time ago. Fear stops you from taking risks and doing things that could harm you. Anger is a signal that someone is overstepping your boundaries and that you need to intervene. Sadness also signals that something is not right; maybe you have lost something or someone important to you. Feeling happy indicates that things are going well and you are enjoying the people or things around you.

Wellbeing is often confused with an absence of fear, sadness and anger, but there is nothing wrong with experiencing any of these emotions; they are all valid and real and each communicates something important. The mindful approach to emotions is to accept them, value them and listen to what they are there to tell you.

'*The word happiness would lose its meaning if it were not balanced by sadness.*'
— **CARL JUNG**

The emotional balloon

We can think of our emotions as an emotional balloon with four openings.

Happiness   Anger

Sadness   Fear

As we go through life, things happen and our emotions are stirred. The pressure in the balloon builds. When enough pressure builds up it needs to be released and it will come out through one of these four openings. The pressure can be released through anger, sadness, fear or happiness.

Young children have all the openings of their emotional balloon wide open, which is why they can experience intense anger, sadness, happiness and even fear in a matter of minutes. As you grow up, some of these openings can become partially or even completely closed. Which openings remain fully open and which become partially or fully closed depends on your personality, the culture you grew up in, significant life events and your upbringing. The extent to which the four openings are open becomes a blueprint for your emotional landscape as an adult. Closing off one or more openings leads to unbalanced reactions because the pressure cannot be released through the appropriate funnel. It builds up and then is redirected to come out through an alternative emotion. Here are some examples.

UPBRINGING

A boy grows up in a family where he is taught that boys don't cry. He learns to see sadness as a sign of weakness, and therefore he completely or partially closes off the opening of sadness.

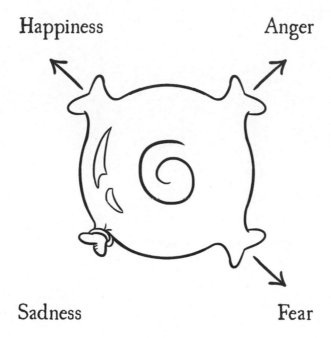

Happiness   Anger

Sadness   Fear

A girl grows up with an anxious mother who constantly expresses her worries and shows very little happiness. The opening of fear becomes wider and wider as this little girl grows up and happiness becomes smaller.

A boy grows up in a family with many struggles; to not be a burden to his parents he adopts the role of the happy child. The opening of happiness becomes wide and the other three become partially or completely closed off.

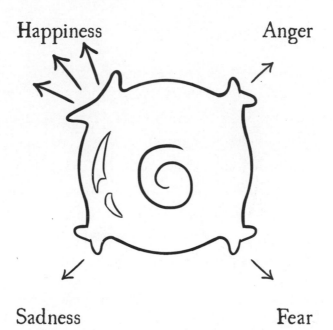

PERSONALITY

An introverted person is more likely to partially or completely close off the 'bigger emotions' — anger and happiness — and to leave open the 'smaller emotions' — fear and sadness. The opposite tendency is likely for an extroverted person.

SIGNIFICANT LIFE EVENTS

Significant life events are events that at the time or afterwards were *experienced* by the person as significant and are often accompanied by a strong emotional response. Events such as losing a loved family member or suffering any type of abuse (physical, emotional or sexual) are always significant events. Events don't always have to be significant for everyone in order to have a deep impact on a child. For example, losing their teddy bear or being frightened by a fire alarm in the absence of parents can be significant events.

A young boy is overwhelmed by fear when the fire alarm goes off while he is with a babysitter. She is unable to calm him down. The opening of fear becomes enlarged and the opening of happiness becomes partially or fully closed.

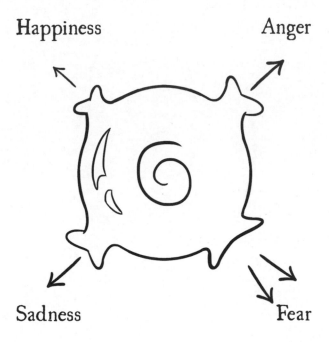

Happiness

Anger

Sadness

Fear

A girl is emotionally and verbally abused in her childhood; sadness and fear become wide open, and happiness becomes partially or completely closed off.

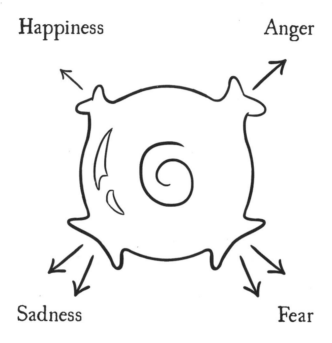

Happiness

Anger

Sadness

Fear

A boy is humiliated by his father when he receives a bad grade in school; both fear and anger become enlarged, and happiness and sadness become smaller.

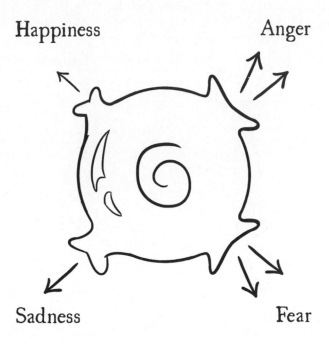

INSIGHT INSPIRATION

1. Take a moment to think about your emotional balloon. Which openings are fully open and which ones are partially or completely closed off? It can help to think of the emotions you feel on a regular basis (open) and the ones you hardly ever feel (closed).

2. What consequences has this emotional blueprint had for you?

3. How has this affected your life and your relationships?

The conscious and the subconscious mind

Your brain requires a lot of energy to operate, so it seeks to conserve energy by using efficient ways of operating. One way it does this is through conscious and subconscious processing. To save brain energy, the brain automates much of what you do, and these become the subconscious processes. Your brain's subconscious processes take care of basic life functions, such as breathing, heart rate and digestion.

The subconscious brain takes care of the fight-or-flight response (stress levels) and learned behaviours and habits. This way you don't have to pay attention to these things; they happen on autopilot. Up to 95 per cent of all processes happen at the subconscious level — and this is a good thing! If all these processes were overcrowding your conscious mind, your system would simply overload.

You can think of your mind as an iceberg, with the conscious mind being the part above the water and the subconscious mind the part below the surface (see illustration on page 54).

THE CONSCIOUS MIND

The things that happen in your conscious mind are the things you are aware of right now, in this moment. Your conscious mind has limited capacity and you can compare your awareness to a spotlight that moves from one thing to another. For example, if you are paying attention to what you are reading, then your present moment awareness is focused on the text of this book.

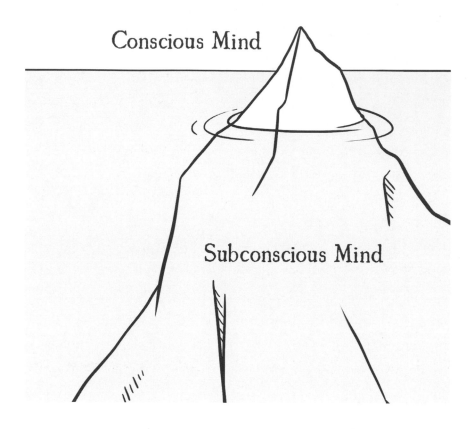

Conscious Mind

Subconscious Mind

If you become distracted by a sound your awareness moves from the text to the sound. If you are distracted by worries your awareness is with the worries rather than the text.

THE SUBCONSCIOUS MIND

The subconscious mind can be divided into two parts. The first part is just beneath the surface and includes all the things that you can relatively easily bring to mind. You can think of it as a library: there are many books but you won't read them all at once. If you need certain information you know where to look for it and you are able to find it and bring it into your immediate consciousness.

The lower part of your subconscious mind consists of the processes that occur automatically and are not readily available for introspection. These include thought processes, memories and feelings. You can think of your subconscious mind as a messy basement with many unopened boxes. They have been stored there a long time ago and you are unaware of what is in them. Even though they exist under the surface of your conscious awareness, these processes impact your conscious thoughts, feelings and behaviours.

Emotions

Now, back to emotions.

When you experience an emotion, there are three options. The emotion can:
- become stuck,
- be suppressed, or
- be processed.

STUCK IN EMOTIONS

When emotions become stuck, you cannot move on from whatever experience triggered that emotion; both your brain and your body remain in an upset state. You know you are stuck in an emotion when you cannot stop thinking about the event that triggered it and you stay emotionally upset for days or even weeks (even if this is on and off). Most of us have experienced this at some stage, and when this state lasts for a long time, serious problems can occur. Being stuck in emotions is accompanied by an overactive red brain and increases the risk of developing depression, an anxiety disorder, issues with sleeping and post-traumatic stress disorder.

Post-traumatic stress disorder is an example of a brain becoming stuck on an event and the emotions it has triggered. In this state the person can experience:

- random flashbacks,
- nightmares,
- continuous high stress levels,
- tensed muscles,
- low mood,
- agitation,
- fear of returning to the place the event happened,
- changed sleep patterns,
- change in appetite.

Here are some examples.

- Your partner just ended the relationship. You cannot think about anything else. You lose your appetite, have trouble sleeping and lack motivation to do anything. You have random flashbacks to the good and the bad times. In your mind you replay the conversations you had countless times without gaining any new insights or resolutions.
- Someone said something unkind to you and you cannot stop thinking about it. Every time you think back to what happened you feel tense, there is a knot in your stomach and you get upset.

Rather than helpful thinking, your thoughts just keep repeating what happened, making you feel more and more upset.

SUPPRESSED EMOTIONS

The second option we have when it comes to emotions is to suppress them. Most people don't like to pay much attention to negative emotions. This can be because you are being hard on yourself ('Don't get upset, it was your own fault!'), or because you think paying attention to the emotion will make it worse instead of better ('Just get over it, it's no big deal.'), or because you have to keep going and don't have the time or opportunity to allow your attention to dwell on your feelings ('I don't have time to be upset, I have a deadline!'). This will lead to suppressing the emotion, which might work in the short term but leads to stress either in the moment or afterwards.

Think back to your emotional balloon and the openings that are partially or completely closed off. The emotions that you have learned to close off do not just disappear; they are transported from the conscious mind to the subconscious mind. You can compare suppressing emotions to pushing a balloon under water: it requires energy, and in time the balloon will just pop up again. The same thing happens with suppressed emotions, they find their way into your thoughts and feelings and are often expressed in messy ways.

Here are some examples.

■ A colleague gives you negative feedback. You keep your frustration in but when you go out for coffee you are unfriendly to the waitress.

■ A mother is frustrated by her child but tries to stay calm and patient. Then her husband comes home and she yells at him over something minor.

■ A child feels intimidated by his new baby brother but is told that he has to be nice to him. He then starts to hit other children.

■ Your employee is not doing a good job. You worry about confronting him but try not to think about it. You go home but instead of engaging you disconnect and withdraw from your partner.

PROCESSING EMOTIONS

The third, and preferred, option of dealing with emotions is to process them. When you process an emotion your brain works through what happened and then stores the information in the library of your brain in a neat and orderly way. Then the event becomes a memory. It might be an unpleasant memory, but when you think back to it you feel calm and remain in control of your thoughts and feelings. All events and emotions can be processed, no matter how horrible they are. Significant events like traumas often take more time to process than small events, but they *can* be fully processed and then stored in the mind's library.

The green brain promotes the processing of emotions while the orange- and red-brain states promote suppressing or becoming stuck in emotions. It is important to realize that you can experience an unpleasant emotion and still be in the green-brain state. The green- or red-brain activity is determined by how you approach the emotion. If you approach it with a kind and non-judgmental attitude you remain in the green zone where processing can take place. When you judge your emotion you move to orange or red and processing is blocked, leaving only the options of suppressing or becoming stuck.

Acknowledge–Link–Let Go

The approach to mindfully processing emotions proposed by therapist Pauline Skeates states that the brain requires three steps to process emotions. The first step is to acknowledge the emotion, the second step is to link the emotion to the trigger and the third step is to let the emotion go.

Step 1: Acknowledge

Your brain cannot process something that you do not acknowledge. In order to be processed, an event and the emotion attached need your kind and non-judgmental attention. This attitude is required to ensure the green-brain state, which is necessary for processing to happen.

One way of acknowledging your emotion is by simply saying 'hello' to it.

Hello feeling nervous.

Hello anger.

Hello stress.

Saying hello to an emotion is a kind and non-judgmental way of acknowledging it and activating the green brain. This process 'separates' you from the emotion, which immediately gives you a different perspective and more control. It reminds you that you are not consumed by this emotion. You are you, and this emotion is a temporary feeling that is here, in this moment. You are not anger; there is you, and you are saying hello to anger. You are not stress; there is you, and you are acknowledging that in this moment stress is also there.

> *'The more comfortably you can acknowledge and accept your emotions the easier they can be processed and diffused.'*
> **— PAULINE SKEATES**

Step 2: Link

The second step in processing an emotion is to link it to the event that caused it. A mindful way to make this link is to say to the emotion: 'It makes perfect sense that you are here given the situation.'

When you say this, either out loud or in your mind, your brain immediately starts to make sense of why that emotion is there. It starts to scan your memory to look for the triggers that caused the emotion, and in this way your attention is brought to these triggers in a calm and non-judgmental way. Give yourself a moment to think about the things that come into your awareness, without judging them or trying to make them any different. Simply notice what comes to your mind and observe these things in a kind and non-judgmental way. In that process the linking is done.

Once you start to practise this skill you will gain important insight into what is triggering your emotions. You can take the linking one step further by saying to the emotion: 'It makes perfect sense that you are here given what I have gone through.'

There are often underlying, unprocessed events that are fuelling your current emotion without you realizing it. When you say to the emotion, 'It makes perfect sense that you are here given what I have gone through,' your brain automatically begins to scan your past for these underlying, unprocessed events. Memories will come up, creating sometimes surprising insights and uncovering links you were not aware of. This often leads to the response, 'I had no idea that past event was linked to why I am feeling this way, but now I see it makes so much sense.'

For most people, gaining insights into links between current emotions and past events gives immediate relief and understanding. This helps in applying the next step.

Step 3: Let go

The last step of processing emotions is letting go. When you let go you are not saying that what happened was okay or that you will let it happen again. You are letting go of the emotions so your brain can store it in the library of your mind and you can move on.

To let go:
■ Put one hand on your chest and one hand on your stomach.
■ Take a deep breath.
■ As you breathe out, relax and drop your shoulders.
■ Say or think, 'I let it go.'
■ Repeat a few times.

Your emotions and physical body are manifestly connected. When you think back to something you have not processed, it will lead to tension in your neck and shoulder area, and your breathing will become shallow. When you consciously take deep breaths and drop your shoulders, you are adjusting your physical body to help your mind process the emotion and let it go.

You can increase the impact of this step by placing one hand on your chest and the other hand on your stomach. When you do this something extraordinary happens in your brain: what we call the social engagement system is activated. This is a combination of brain areas that become active in meaningful social interaction. By placing one hand on your chest and one on your stomach, you are activating the same brain activity that is activated when you are holding the hand of a loved one.

Research shows that when the social engagement system is activated, people feel more secure and confident. They also assess situations as less challenging. By adding this simple step to the Acknowledge–Link–Let Go (ALL) technique you are offering yourself emotional support and encouragement, as well as increasing your green-brain activity and the effectiveness of the exercise.

What if Acknowledge–Link–Let Go doesn't work?

Some emotions are processed after doing this exercise only once. Others take more time. This often depends on how strong the emotion is. Every time you do this exercise you are taking a step in processing the event and emotion.

WHAT IF IT TRIGGERS ANOTHER UNPLEASANT EMOTION?

With more significant events you will often find that once you have processed one emotion you may encounter another. When you do, just repeat the steps with this new emotion that has come to your awareness. Once you feel calm and peaceful and can look back at what happened without your emotions being stirred again, you have fully processed the event and the emotion.

Here are some examples.

LINKING TO THE SITUATION

Stuck in stress (red brain): Jenny is running late and feels stressed. She thinks to herself, 'What is wrong with me, why can't I ever be on time?! I am definitely going to be late now. I can't believe it, I am so bad at planning!' She feels stressed, her breathing is shallow and her muscles are tense.

Processing stress (green brain): Jenny is running late and feels stressed. She says to the emotion, 'Hello stress. It makes perfect sense that you are here, because I am late and I hate being late.'

Then she breathes out, drops her shoulders and says, 'I let it go.' Her breathing becomes deeper, her muscles relax and she feels calm and in control again.

Stuck in anger (red brain): Dan is confronted by his boss in an inconsiderate way. He thinks, 'This guy is such an arrogant bastard, he doesn't even know what he's talking about!' He feels angry, his breathing becomes shallow and his muscles are tense.

Processing frustration (green brain): Dan is confronted by his boss in an inconsiderate way. He processes his anger by thinking, 'Hello anger, it makes perfect sense that you are here. My boss's behaviour is making me angry, and it's a repeat of past occasions when he has acted in the same way.' He then breathes out, drops his shoulders and tries to let go of the anger. After repeating this a few times he feels calm and in control again. Then he can come up with helpful, assertive ways to address the situation.

LINKING TO THE PAST

Stuck in frustration (red brain): Katherine becomes very frustrated when her partner does not respond quickly enough when she asks him something. She thinks, 'Why is he not listening when I speak to him? It is so disrespectful!' This makes her feel even more frustrated and she shouts, 'Why don't you listen to me!' An argument is the result.

Processing frustration (green brain): Katherine becomes very frustrated when her partner does not respond quickly enough when she asks him something. She says to herself, 'Hello frustration, it makes perfect sense that you are here given what I have gone through.' Then the memory of her father often ignoring her comes into her mind and she realizes that her intense frustration with her partner is fuelled by the buried frustration of being ignored by her father. She takes a few deep breaths, relaxes her shoulders and lets it go. When she has calmed down she reminds herself that her partner is not like her father. This makes her want to connect to her partner instead of becoming angry.

Stuck in insecurity (red brain): Alex becomes filled with self-doubt at work and feels nervous and insecure at meetings. He thinks, 'I don't have the right skills to do this job, I am such a failure and will let everyone down.' His self-esteem and mood quickly drop, negatively impacting his ability to think and perform. When he comes home all he thinks about is work and he isolates himself from his family more and more.

Processing insecurity (green brain): Alex becomes filled with self-doubt at work and feels nervous and insecure at meetings. He thinks, 'Hello insecurity, it makes perfect sense that you are here given what I have gone through.' Memories of his demanding father telling him he was a failure when he did not excel come to his mind. He takes a deep breath, drops his shoulders and thinks to himself, 'I let it go, I don't have to please my father anymore and I am not a failure.' His system calms down, he regains his focus and does not give in to the feeling or the need to work until late in the evening but instead he spends quality time with his family.

A mindful approach to emotions

Emotions are not always pleasant or comfortable but they are important because they are part of your brain's messaging system. When you suppress emotions you miss the message your brain is giving you. When you become stuck in an emotion you react out of an emotion-driven impulse, which often does more harm than good. But emotions don't have to automatically put you in the orange or red zone — luckily there is a mindful alternative. A green-brain approach to emotions is to process them, take them seriously and listen to them. When you process the emotion your system calms down, allowing you to effectively respond. In this calm, mindful state you can see clearly and you can actually address the situation in a healthy and effective way.

> *Processing emotions moves you from reactive to responsive.*

EXERCISE 4:
FEELING BETTER

Step 1. Turn your attention to the emotion you are feeling.

Step 2. Say 'hello' to the emotion.

For example, *Hello stress. Hello feeling small. Hello being upset.*

Step 3. Tell the emotion: 'It makes perfect sense that you are here given the situation.'

Step 4. Take a moment to notice what comes to your mind. Stay kind and non-judgmental as you do this, allowing anything that comes to your mind, welcoming it and noticing it, without trying to change it or figure it out.

Step 5. Put one hand on your chest and one hand on your stomach.

Step 6. Take five deep breaths. As you breathe out, relax your shoulders and say to yourself: 'I let it go.'

Step 7. Notice what you are becoming aware of.

 On-the-run tip: *This technique works for processing emotions as they arise, as well as after the fact. Just think back to the situation that upset you and follow the same steps.*

Chapter 4:
MINDFUL CONNECTION TO OTHERS

Feeling connected to others is at the core of what makes you happy. Your brain is wired to want and seek connection with others because this connection provides safety on many levels. But relationships can be challenging and we often become emotionally disconnected from the ones we love; all it takes is a bit of stress, a busy agenda or a misplaced comment. When you become disconnected from the people you love, it greatly affects your happiness and theirs.

You can be in a room full of people but feel completely disconnected, or you can be all by yourself yet feel incredibly connected to the people in your life. Connection is not being around people, it is feeling that someone cares. In this chapter we will look into how mindfulness can be applied to communication and how you can use mindful communication to avoid emotional disconnection and strengthen your bond with the people you love most.

Mindfulness in communication

You are practising mindfulness when you pay attention to what is happening, and you observe it in a kind and non-judgmental way. When you apply this to social interaction it means being present with other people, accepting them and their experience as it is for them, in that moment.

As researcher Brené Brown beautifully puts it in her message on empathy verses sympathy: 'Theresa Wiseman, a nursing scholar, researched empathy and came up with four qualities of empathy. The first one is perspective-taking, the ability to take the perspective of another person or recognize *their* perspective as *their* truth. This involves avoiding judgment, which is not easy when you enjoy it as much as most of us do, and recognizing emotion in other people and then communicating that.' Brown describes empathy as a sacred space and a dynamic that fuels connection. The opposite of empathy is sympathy. Sympathy fuels disconnection even though it often comes from good intentions. Sympathy is when someone shares something with you that is incredibly painful and you respond with the words 'at least'.

'I had a miscarriage . . .'
'At least you know you can get pregnant.'

'John is being kicked out of school . . .'
'At least Sarah is an A student.'

'My marriage is falling apart . . .'
'At least, you have a marriage.'

We do this all the time. We try to make people feel better by redirecting their attention to more positive things. The truth is, it doesn't work. Failing to acknowledge their emotions merely fuels disconnection. Empathy, or mindful connection, happens when you learn to accept other people's uncomfortable emotions; when you stop trying to fix it but create space for whatever they are feeling in that moment. Mindful connection is not trying to pull the other person out of the darkness they are in, it is climbing down and joining them in their experience.

This does not mean that you should never try to cheer anyone up or that you should not give advice. It also does not mean that because you accept their feelings you also have to accept all of their behaviour. You can still address things, but if you first connect, whatever you will do after that will have more effect.

	GREEN BRAIN	RED BRAIN
Underlying constructs	Safe In control/calm	Unsafe Fight-or-flight/stress
Observations	Open view Taking perspective	Fixed point of view Only see your perspective
Attitude	Kind manner Open	Unkind manner Closed
Thinking	Non-judgmental Seeing details/ nuances	Judgmental Black/white
Risk of conflict	Low	High

Let me refresh your memory regarding the red brain and the green brain. As you can see in the table above, a brain in the green zone feels safe and therefore calm and in control. This brain state allows you to see details and nuances and allows you to take another person's perspective. The green brain promotes a kind manner and non-judgmental thinking, which leads to a low risk of conflict. At the opposite end of the spectrum is the red brain. A brain in the red zone feels unsafe. This activates the stress (fight-or-flight) response, putting the brain and body in the best possible state to run or fight but the worst possible state to communicate. In this state a fixed point of view is activated; you only have eyes for the thing that is causing you stress, with no room in your mind for anything else. Taking someone else's perspective becomes hard. Your thinking becomes black-and-white and you are likely to adopt an unkind and judgmental attitude. Until the other person has moved out of the red zone, communication is usually ineffective. Someone who is overwhelmed with emotion or stress won't be able to take on board much of what you have to say.

Very often people in a relationship want the exact same thing, whether it is a love relationship, a parent–child relationship or a work relationship. Both parties need to be heard, to be acknowledged and to have their emotions validated. These are the core principals of connection. Why? Because making someone feel heard, acknowledged and validated is a powerful way to activate *their* green brain. Because mindful connection meets these needs it automatically moves the other person's brain out of the red zone. Creating a safe space for their emotions helps diffuse them so quickly that you will see the person changing within minutes, sometimes even seconds.

Putting mindful connection into practice — Mirror–Link–Pause

Your verbal and non-verbal communication is the most powerful tool that you have to achieve mindful connection. The easiest way of explaining this mindful communication technique is by looking at our interactions with children. Children's emotions are big and clear to see, and because of this your response to them will be easy to identify.

Think about a young child; this can be your own child, a child you know, or an imaginary child. Picture them standing in front of you with a big smile and twinkly eyes and showing you a drawing that they made for you. As you are picturing this, notice what happens to your posture and facial expression. Do you feel a tendency to come down to their level? To raise your eyebrows, to smile and react in a way that echoes their enthusiasm? For most people the answer will be yes. As humans our automatic response to another person's happiness is to *mirror* their facial expressions and their posture. Because children have such strong emotions and show them in such a clear way, the effect will be even clearer than if you were talking to an adult. When you mirror the child's happiness they will feel heard, acknowledged and validated.

Then your attention is likely to move from the child to the drawing. You will look at it and ask questions about it and comment on how beautiful it is. This step is called the *link*. You are making a link between the happiness of the child and the thing that they are so happy and excited about. For example:

Pause

When you *link* the happiness to the drawing, the child feels that you really notice and appreciate whatever they are feeling happy about. This shows the child that you understand why they are feeling happy.

After the mirroring and linking comes the *pause*. The pause does two things. First, it allows the child's brain to really take in your response. Second, it gives the child the opportunity to initiate the next step. This prevents the child from feeling rushed or cut off. When given this time, it usually doesn't take long for the child to easily and comfortably move on to the next thing.

MIRROR–LINK–PAUSE WITH SADNESS

Now think of the same child, standing right in front of you. This time the child is crying. Tears are streaming down their face, their eyebrows are frowning and the corners of their mouth are pointing downwards. While you watch this image in your mind, do you notice a tendency to make a sad face yourself? This *mirrors* their facial expression and is the first step in the Mirror–Link–Pause process we have just discussed. A likely response to a crying child is the question, 'What happened?' Imagine the child pointing to their knee and telling you, 'I fell and hurt my knee.' You are now likely to focus on the knee, to look at it and examine how serious the fall was. By doing this you *link* the emotion to the trigger.

Often parents respond to their crying child by saying: 'You are fine, see, it's really not that bad.' This response is intended to make the child feel better but because it does not follow the Mirror–Link–Pause sequence it does not work. Just imagine that you have come home after a horrible day at work; you feel so awful that you could burst into tears, and when you reach out to your partner they simply say, 'You are fine, see, it's really not that bad.' How would you feel? What would you think? In situations like these, when your emotion is not mirrored and linked, your processing of the emotion will likely be blocked. When that happens there are only two options left: either you become stuck in the emotion or you suppress the emotion.

A young child's brain has not fully developed yet and they are not able to properly process their own emotions. When you tell them they are 'fine' when they are clearly upset, you are emotionally disconnecting from them and robbing them of the opportunity to process their emotion. Then they can only suppress the emotion or become stuck in the emotion, and the option they choose will mostly depend on their temperament and upbringing.

So, how do you help a child (or adult) who is upset to link their emotion to the trigger? You simply ask them, 'What happened?' When they explain the situation to you, you listen and then repeat it back to them, staying very close to the words they used. This is called using *clean language*. For example:

Some people fear that responding in this way will only make the child (or the adult) more upset. The truth is that it most often calms them down very quickly. Even if the other person does not calm down immediately, they are just letting air out of their emotional balloon, and that's a good thing! In mindful communication the goal is not to restore calm as quickly as possible, it is to offer connection so the person's emotion can be processed without suppression, allowing the green brain to take over again. When you Mirror–Link–Pause, you are offering connection. The other person will feel heard, validated and cared for by your response, which allows their brain to process the emotion they are feeling and return to a green-brain state where they can move on from what happened. When this process is facilitated in a child, they learn how to process their own emotions using Acknowledge–Link–Let Go, which is the individual version of Mirror-Link-Pause.

MIRROR–LINK–PAUSE WITH ANGER

Again, imagine the same child standing right in front of you. This time they are frowning heavily and looking very angry. The child yells at you, 'Johnny took my toy again!' Common responses of parents include, 'Well, you can find another toy to play with,' or, 'It's good to be able to share,' or, 'When he is finished with it you can have it again, just play with something else in the meantime.' Now, imagine for a moment that someone comes along and just takes your phone without asking and refuses to give it back. How would you feel? What would you think? Then imagine that when you go to the authorities in order to get it back, they respond with, 'Just find something else to play with.' How would this response make you feel? To a child a toy has the same value that your phone has to you.

Because this response does not follow the Mirror–Link–Pause sequence, it does not allow for emotions to be processed. The angry child then has two options left. The first option is to become stuck in the anger. When the child becomes even angrier because the conditions to process the emotion are not facilitated, they risk being told off and emotionally rejected by their parent. For example:

The other option the child has is to suppress the anger. Suppressed emotions lead to increased stress. In children this can lead to issues such as trouble sleeping, fears, tantrums, refusing to eat, nightmares and trouble concentrating.

To avoid this and encourage the child to process the emotion, the adult can mirror, link and then pause. For example:

Mirror

Link and Pause

Link and Pause

Move On

Mirror–Link–Pause works well with both children and adults. You simply adjust your verbal and non-verbal language to match the age of the person you are talking to.

Here are a few examples given by course participants.

'I applied this technique to my husband when he was really upset about a leakage in the house. He said, "That's it, we're selling this house!" Usually I would have told him to just calm down and that no, we are not selling the house. This time, I applied Mirror–Link–Pause and said, "I know, it's terribly frustrating that we keep having these problems!" It felt like we were on the same team and he calmed down straightaway. After only a few minutes he no longer wanted to sell the house, and we came up with a good solution to the problem.'

'My boss often becomes stressed and then he starts to make unrealistic demands. Instead of joining him in the state of stress, I stayed calm and said, "It's so stressful when clients make all these demands." This calmed him down and we were able to discuss the issue and come up with a plan.'

'As a teacher I found this technique especially helpful with special-needs children. At school we have an autistic child who fixates on spots on her clothing. Instead of reassuring her that there are no spots on her shirt I said to her, "Those spots are really bothering you." To my surprise she then calmed down and moved on very quickly.'

THE PAUSE IN MIRROR–LINK–PAUSE

The importance of the pause is often overlooked. The pause creates space for the mirroring and the linking to have its effect on the other person's brain. This doesn't have to take longer than a few seconds, but these few seconds are important. It is hard for the brain to process something when it has to also listen to what you are saying.

Giving it a few seconds of silence allows the brain to process the emotion. Many people feel uncomfortable with a silence, but it is important to realize that the pause might be uncomfortable for you but it is not for the other person.

Usually the change in eye gaze and posture happens during the pause. Often there is a noticeable out-breath and relaxation of the shoulders and a shift to acceptance and solution-based language. For example:

Friend: 'I haven't had a good night's sleep in weeks. Jane is driving me nuts!'

You: 'That must be exhausting.'

Friend: 'Yes it is.'

Pause.

Friend: (sighing) 'I guess it won't be this way forever, though.'

You: 'No, it won't last forever.'

Partner: 'I thought you would cook tonight. You need to let me know in advance if you change your plans!'

You: 'I'm sorry. I can imagine it's frustrating for you if I change my plans and forget to tell you.'

Partner: 'Yes it is!'

Pause.

Partner: (sighing) 'Okay, we'll just order a takeaway, but next time please let me know on time.'

CLEAN LANGUAGE

Using clean language will make the Mirror–Link–Pause technique more effective. Clean language means that you use words the other person has used or something very similar. This helps them to focus on their emotions instead of making sure you understand how they feel. For example:

No clean language

Colleague: 'I am so annoyed with Jim.'

You: 'You're angry with Jim?'

Colleague: 'Not angry, just annoyed.'

Clean language

Colleague: 'I am so annoyed with Jim.'

You: 'You're annoyed with Jim?'

Colleague: 'Yes I am, he keeps changing his mind and giving me more work!'

You: 'That *is* annoying.'

No clean language

Friend: 'I really don't know what I've done wrong.'

You: 'You must feel so sad.'

Friend: 'I feel more confused, because I can't figure out what I've done wrong.'

Clean language

Friend: 'I really don't know what I've done wrong.'

You: 'You think you've done something wrong but you don't know what?'

Friend: 'Yes, exactly! I just can't figure it out.'

If the person does not tell you how they are feeling, it is fine to make assumptions based on their body language and their story. As you can see in the above examples, the other person will correct you if you get it wrong. For example:

Friend: 'Sarah is flunking school, I just got a call from her teacher.'

You: 'How upsetting.' Or 'I can imagine you feel very upset.' Or 'That must be very upsetting.'

Friend: 'Yes it is.'

Client: 'I was driving and all of a sudden a car was coming at me and he was in my lane. I don't know how it got there. The next thing I knew there was a big crash.'

Therapist: 'How scary.' Or 'That must have been very scary.' Or 'I can imagine you were feeling very scared.'

Client: 'Yes it was.'

Whenever you reflect back the emotion, you are encouraging the other person to focus on the emotional side of the situation. When you use clean language to reflect back the factual side of their story, you are encouraging them to elaborate on that. For example:

Focus on the facts

Colleague: 'My boss is so stressed it's driving me crazy!'

You: 'Your boss is stressed?'

Colleague: 'Yes, he runs around like a headless chicken and keeps adding things to my list that are not even my responsibility.'

Focus on the emotion

Colleague: 'My boss is so stressed it's driving me crazy!'

You: 'It's driving you crazy?'

Colleague: 'Yes, I'm getting really stressed too because of the way he's behaving.'

Focus on the facts

Client: (looking upset) 'It has been a difficult week.'

Therapist: 'A difficult week?'

Client: 'Yes, Shaun left me on Monday.'

Focus on the emotion

Client: (looking upset) 'It has been a difficult week.'

Therapist: 'You seem very upset.'

Client: 'Yes, I am. Very upset. I just don't know what to do.'

You can use both approaches in the same conversation — just remember that the other person will be inclined to elaborate on that which you reflect back with clean language. When people stick to the facts rather than the emotion underlying the situation, it can be helpful to focus on the emotional side using clean language. This allows for the facts to be discussed as well as for the emotion to be processed.

HOW TO USE MIRROR–LINK–PAUSE

This technique does not replace what you would normally do, whether it be setting boundaries for a child or offering solutions or encouragement to a friend or colleague; it is an 'add on' to calm down another person's brain so that your next step will be more effective.

> *'Connect before you direct.'*
> **— DANIEL SIEGEL**

For example: setting boundaries.

A child has hit another child.

Mirror

Link

Link and Pause

Boundary Setting

What if Mirror–Link–Pause doesn't work?

When you apply this technique to people who are very close to you and have known you for a long time, there is a chance they will respond to the change in your approach rather than the technique. They may even feel like you are making fun of them. To avoid this it is important to start by making small changes to your interactions. You can see your way of communicating with them as a dance: you have been dancing the same dance for years, and if you change the steps all of a sudden it can be confusing and may even feel unsafe for the other person. Their initial response will be to pull you back into the familiar routine. If you can make the changes subtle enough, you *can* change the dance into a better one without triggering resistance. Also remember that changing patterns is not easy, it comes with practice and it comes with time. If the technique doesn't work all at once, don't give up; evaluate and try again.

WHAT IF THE PERSON BECOMES MORE UPSET?

If a person — adult or child — becomes more emotional when you apply the Mirror–Link–Pause technique it is probably because you are creating space for their emotions, which invites them to blow off steam. Remember that this is a healthy and necessary step to processing emotions. When someone becomes overwhelmed you can pause and just give them a big hug, or you can calm them down by having them focus on something else and then come back to the topic at a later time.

WHAT IF ANOTHER EMOTION COMES UP?

We all have different layers of emotions. Frustration and anger often show up first. When you use the Mirror–Link–Pause technique you can help someone process the first layer of emotion; after that, the underlying emotion will come up. Often this is sadness or fear. When this happens, just follow the steps again. When you can notice physical relaxation and the move to acceptance and problem-solving language, you know that the emotions have been processed.

Integrate

The way I have described the technique is very black-and-white. In real life you will naturally mix the technique up with your own way of communicating. The idea is to practise the technique and then integrate it into your communication in a way that works well for you. In time you will notice that you leave more space for other people's emotions and stop trying to fix them or make them feel better by distracting them with *At least* . . . You will notice that mindful connection happens when you can accept their uncomfortable emotions and be understanding and non-judgmental about them. Offering the reassurance that the way they are feeling makes perfect sense in the situation is more powerful than offering solutions. You are respectfully facilitating the processing of their own emotions, without cutting the process short. When you allow this to happen you will witness the way people visibly shift from the red- to the green-brain state and start to come up with great solutions themselves — solutions that you could have never thought of.

INSIGHT INSPIRATION

When someone around you is feeling a negative emotion, how do you usually respond? Do you tell them *At least* . . . ? Do you give advice? Do you try to come up with solutions or suggestions?

With whom would you like to have more mindful connection?

How would this person feel if you validated their emotions without rushing solutions? How would that change your interactions with them?

EXERCISE 5:
MINDFULLY PROCESSING ANOTHER'S EMOTIONS

Mirror

Step 1. Mirror the facial expression and body posture of the other person.

Step 2. Acknowledge their emotion. For example:

- How upsetting/annoying/stressful/sad/etc.
- I can see that you feel very upset/annoyed/stressed/sad/etc.
- You must be feeling upset/annoyed/stressed/sad/etc.

Link

Step 3. Link the emotion to the trigger. For example:

- What happened?
- Tell me more.

Step 4. Use clean language to mention the trigger as they described it.

Pause

Step 5. Pause for a few seconds.

If the person still seems emotional: repeat **steps 1 to 5**.

If another emotion comes up: repeat **steps 1 to 5**.

If they stay on a factual level: focus on mirroring the emotion.

Once you see the change in eye gaze, posture and language to acceptance and problem-solving language, the emotion has been processed.

 On-the-run tip: *Use 'clean language' in everyday situations, even when the person you are speaking with is not upset. It will improve the connection because it makes them feel like you really get what they are saying.*

Chapter 5:
THE POWER OF THOUGHTS

The way you navigate through life largely depends on your thoughts. They determine how you feel, your decisions and your actions — every part of your life that you can control. Your thinking is one of the most powerful tools you will ever have in changing your life. Let me explain why.

The Cognitive Behavioural Therapy (CBT) model is one of the most important models in psychology. This model states that events lead to thoughts, thoughts lead to feelings, feelings to behaviours, and behaviours have consequences. It is not the events themselves that determine how you feel and behave; it is the *thoughts you have about these events* that trigger the sequence of feelings, behaviours and consequences. As with every model, it is a simplification of a complex and dynamic reality. However, it is a very useful tool that gives insight into how the mind works.

COGNITIVE BEHAVIOURAL THERAPY MODEL

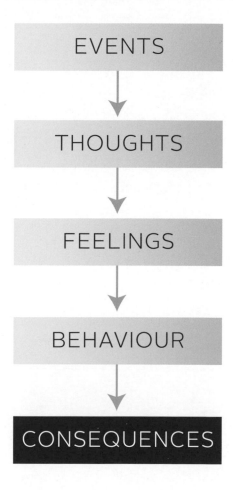

Here are some examples of the CBT model.

Example 1

Scenario 1

Event	You are standing on a stage, about to give a presentation. You look out into the room and see a large group of people. Your heart begins to beat faster and your hands become sweaty.
Thought	Then you think, 'Oh no, what a large group. I can't do this!'
Feelings	You feel anxious, nervous and insecure.
Behaviour	You forget the words, make mistakes and speak too quickly.
Consequence	Your performance is less than it could have been and you feel bad about it afterwards.

Scenario 2

Event	You are standing on a stage, about to give a presentation. You look out into the room and see a large group of people. Your heart begins to beat faster and your hands become sweaty.
Thought	Then you think, 'Oh wow, what a large group. This is going to be great!'
Feelings	You feel energized, confident and excited.
Behaviour	You speak with confidence and remember your text, and your enthusiasm is noticeable.
Consequence	Your performance is great and you feel happy and satisfied afterwards.

The event is the same, but different thoughts about the event lead to completely different outcomes. In the first scenario you perceive the event as threatening, activating the red brain, which makes it hard to perform well. In the second scenario your thoughts are non-threatening, activating the orange or green brain, which both promote good performance.

Another example. Let's say you are lying in bed and you suddenly hear a loud bang. This is an event. If you then think to yourself 'It is a burglar' you will probably feel scared. Your personality and past experiences will determine your actions, but let's say you 'freeze'. You feel scared and hide under the blankets — a likely consequence of this is that it will take a long time for you to fall asleep and you will feel tired the next day.

Example 2

Scenario 1

Event	You are lying in bed and you hear a loud bang.
Thought	Then you think, 'It's a burglar!'
Feelings	You feel scared and vulnerable.
Behaviour	You freeze and hide under the blankets.
Consequence	You lie awake for hours, and after eventually falling into a restless sleep you feel tired and cranky the next day.

Scenario 2

Event	You are lying in bed and you hear a loud bang.
Thought	Then you think, 'It's just the neighbour's cat.'
Feelings	You feel relieved.
Behaviour	You relax and fall asleep.
Consequence	You get a good night's sleep and wake up the following morning feeling rested.

Again, the exact same event can have two completely different outcomes. The outcome does not depend on the event but on *your thoughts about the event*. In the first scenario the red brain is activated because your mind perceives a threat when thinking the sound is made by a burglar. This perceived threat activates the stress response and in this situation the triggered emotion is fear. In the second scenario, the same event has a very different outcome. The thought about the event is a non-threatening, non-judgmental one, therefore it activates the green brain. This leads to feeling relieved, relaxed and having a good night's sleep.

These examples show that it is your interpretation (i.e. what you think is going on), that activates either the green or the red brain. This is important because often you cannot change your situation or circumstances but you are able to change your thoughts and therefore create a very different outcome, even if the situation remains unchanged.

Science

An eight-year study by the University of Wisconsin-Madison shows that if you have been under a lot of stress in the past 12 months the risk of premature death increases by 43 per cent. One of the most interesting findings is that this was found to be true only for the people who also *believed* that stress was harmful to their health. People who experienced significant stress but did not see stress as harmful were no more likely to die prematurely. In fact, they had the lowest risk of premature death, even lower than the people in the study who experienced little stress! When you view stress symptoms such as increased heart rate, breathing and that adrenaline rush as positive signs that your body is getting ready to meet a challenge, there seems to be no negative effect on your health.

In a study conducted by Harvard University, researchers told participants with induced stress to view their increased heart rate as a sign their body was getting ready to perform, and their change in breathing as a helpful response because the body was pumping more oxygen to the brain. When participants started to see these stress symptoms as helpful they became less stressed and anxious and more confident. When participants viewed their stress symptoms as positive their heart rate increased but their blood vessels did not become narrow (a combination associated with a normal stress response); instead, the vessels stayed relaxed. This state of increased heart rate combined with relaxed blood vessels resembles the body's response in moments of joy and courage. In the usual stress response, increased heart rate combined with narrowed blood vessels leads to an unhealthy state that increases the risk of cardiovascular disease.

These studies and others like it tell us that when you change your mind about stress, you can change your physical response to stress. If you control your thoughts and keep them neutral or positive, you can use the stress response and turn it into a moment of joy and confidence rather than a moment of fear and stress. Over time this could mean the difference between a stress-induced heart attack leading to premature death or living a long and healthy life.

Core beliefs

When you are thinking stressful thoughts they are part of your conscious mind. But they don't stand on their own. They are a result of what is happening in your subconscious mind. Your subconscious mind contains many different things including memories, feelings and thoughts, and at the very 'bottom' of your subconscious mind are what we call the core beliefs. These are beliefs you hold about yourself and the world, and about what you have to do in order to be 'okay'. Established in early childhood, core beliefs are the fundamental building blocks of your thoughts and, therefore, your feelings.

Because your core beliefs are part of your subconscious mind, they are not always readily available for introspection. They are like glasses through which you see the world and the events that

CORE BELIEFS

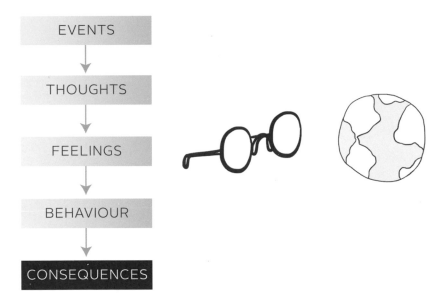

EVENTS

↓

THOUGHTS

↓

FEELINGS

↓

BEHAVIOUR

↓

CONSEQUENCES

happen in your life — the only issue is, most people don't know they are wearing these glasses. Therefore your belief about the world *is* as you *see* the world, not realizing it might be your dark or rose-tinted glasses colouring what you see. Naturally, therefore, you project your core beliefs about yourself and the world onto everything you see and believe that you are seeing things clearly and accurately. This is reinforced because your core beliefs *feel* so strong and so true.

For example, one client had the core belief that she was not good enough and that no one liked her. As soon as she walked into a room full of people she would convince herself that no one there liked her and that they did not want her to be there. She was projecting her thoughts and feelings onto the people in the room,

It's such a dark place out there.

It's such a happy place out there.

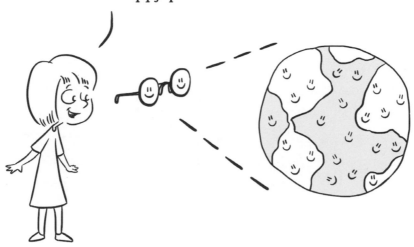

looking through her glasses and believing that what she saw were the thoughts and feelings of these other people. This feeling was so strong and felt so true that she never questioned it; she just accepted it as the truth.

In time a core belief can become a self-fulfilling prophecy; something that becomes true not because it was originally true but because people respond to your behaviour, which comes from the belief that it is true. In this example my client became insecure and withdrawn when she was around other people. This stopped her from being her usual fun and loving self. Instead she would be quiet and try to find an excuse to leave as soon as possible. Because of this behaviour, in time people started to think that *she* did not like *them* very much and that she did not want to be there. They probably started to see her as withdrawn, cold and not very much fun to be around, which led to her not being invited to events. In this way, her core belief came full circle and actually turned into the reality.

Another example is a client who had a core belief that the world is a dangerous place. This made him constantly on edge and vigilant (overactive red brain), and his mind was constantly looking for evidence that he was right. He planned his every action by calculating risks. To him this way of living made perfect sense, because the belief *felt* so true and rational. However, he did suffer from chronic stress, digestive issues, relationship difficulties and had trouble sleeping. These were likely a result of his overactive red brain and chronic high stress. In time this could turn into a self-fulfilling prophecy: because of his high stress level and lack of sleep he might be unable to focus well or see the bigger picture, which would make him more prone to making mistakes. This could then lead to dangerous situations.

'Thoughts become things.'
— UNKNOWN

THE ORIGIN OF CORE BELIEFS

Core beliefs are formed early on in life, and they are a result of the emotional environment you grew up in. Significant life events and your personality also play a big role in shaping your core beliefs.

Because core beliefs are formed when you are still a young child, they are formed with a child's brain and therefore depict child-like thinking, which can be characterized as black-and-white and all-or-nothing thinking. Core beliefs are often very self-centred because this is the way children see the world. A child always believes it is 'all about them'. When their parent is angry they don't have the brain capacity yet to see the bigger picture and think 'Mum is just having a bad day today, this is not because of me.' Instead they will automatically assume it *is* because of them.

Core beliefs can be positive, neutral or negative. Examples of positive core beliefs are *I am okay, I am loved* or *I am smart.* A common negative core belief is *I am not good enough.* This is a very judgmental and black-and-white thought that leaves no room for nuance; it focuses completely on the person holding the core belief. It is unspecific and therefore can be applied to any situation. It is a common core belief for people who grew up with conditional love or unpredictable love and acceptance.

Other common core beliefs are *I am bad* or *It is my fault.* Again these thoughts are very black-and-white, all-or-nothing, self-centred and unspecific. These or similar core beliefs are common for people who grew up with an abusive, dismissive or emotionally unavailable parent. Because children completely depend on their parents or caregivers for food, shelter and emotional care, children are incredibly loyal to their parents or caregivers. Emotionally rejecting the parent would endanger their chances of survival, so a child's brain is programmed to stay emotionally loyal to the parent no matter what. The only way to stay loyal to a dismissive, abusive or (emotionally) neglectful parent is to believe that you deserve to be treated this way and side *with* the parent. This is how the core belief *I am bad* or *I am not good enough* is founded.

One client had a powerful insight during a mindfulness exercise. In her mind, she was taken back to a situation that happened when she was only eight years old when her father had touched her inappropriately. After the event she was in the kitchen with her family sitting around the kitchen table when she mentioned what had happened. Then her father looked at *her* in disgust with both fear and anger showing on his face. Because she was only a child she had no choice but to stay emotionally loyal to her father, because it would render her unsafe to lose the 'acceptance' of the adult on whom she was completely dependent. Therefore, in that moment, her negative thoughts and feelings about her father flipped around and became directed at herself. She decided that there must be something wrong with *her*; she started to believe that *she* was disgusting and bad. She agreed with the adult because to a child's brain, disagreeing is unsafe. The sad consequence is that in that moment, when her core beliefs *I am bad* and *There is something wrong with me* were born, her internal world became unsafe.

The link

When a home situation is filled with negative dynamics and emotions, a child will pick up on them. This aligns with step 1 of the Acknowledge–Link–Let Go (ALL) theory of processing emotions. The child might not be able to consciously acknowledge and name the emotions, but on a subconscious level they pick up on tension very quickly (step 1: Acknowledge). The child's brain will then automatically look for the link (step 2: Link). The correct response would be to link the negative emotion to the parent — after all, it is the parent who is responsible for these negative dynamics, the child is just a child and can never be held responsible. But because in a child's brain the world revolves around them and it is dangerous to be emotionally disloyal to their parents, they are more likely to link the negative emotion to themselves. So, when you yell or scream or argue with your partner in the presence of your child, the child will pick up on the negative emotion (step 1: Acknowledge), and because of the way their brain works, they are likely to link it to themselves (step 2: Link). The child will see themselves as the cause of the negative emotion and when this is an ongoing dynamic, core beliefs such as *I am bad* or *It is my fault* are created.

For example, one of my clients has two sons: an adult son and a little boy who was aged three at the time. The eldest son had drug issues and was in trouble with the law. Understandably this led to anger and tension in the house. The three-year-old boy picked up on these negative dynamics, and within the course of a week he went from being a happy and content young boy (green-brain state) to a sad, withdrawn child. He started to say things like, 'I am useless' and 'Everyone is angry with me' (red-brain state). Of course this upset the parents and they tried to explain that they were not angry with him but they did not want to burden him with the knowledge of what was going on with his brother. They told him that everything was fine and they were not angry with him. This was not effective, because everything was not fine, and denying the tension or even acknowledging it without offering a link did not relieve the child from linking the emotions to himself.

After the mother learned the ALL technique, they changed their approach from telling the child that everything was fine (which it was not) to acknowledging that 'Yes, Mummy and Daddy are really angry' (step 1. Acknowledge). Then they offered a link that was understandable to a three-year-old by pointing out that his older brother had parked his car on the grass leaving marks. They said, 'We are really angry with your brother because he parked his car on the grass and cars belong on the road. Look, the lawn is very damaged!' The mother described how in that moment her son became silent and thought deeply for a few seconds. She could see the 'aha moment' on his face when he dropped his shoulders and he said, 'Yes, Mummy, it was very naughty of him to park his car on the grass, cars belong on the road not on the grass!' After that he went back to being his normal self. He was now able to link the negative emotions to something the older brother had done (linking to an action is always better than linking to a person) and therefore he could understand, process and let go. In this example we gain a rare insight into a three-year-old's way of thinking and how children link negative emotions to themselves when there is no clear trigger to link them to.

When parents say things like, 'You are so slow,' 'What is wrong with you?' or 'I am not happy with you,' they offer links the child remembers and continues to use even into adulthood. The way your parents made you feel either by what they said or what they did becomes part of your subconscious thoughts and core beliefs, and these in turn shape your conscious thoughts and your internal dialogue — your self-talk. In psychology this part is often referred to as the internal critical parent. The internal critical parent is a part of the adult that continues the trend the parents have started. I believe that this process is at the core of why so many people are unduly hard on themselves.

Why are core beliefs important?

Gaining insight into your core beliefs and understanding their origins helps you to identify and understand the glasses you are wearing. This insight allows your mind to open up to the possibility that things might not *be* true even when they *feel* true. Something is not true just because it feels true; it could be your glasses, your projections, that you are seeing rather than reality.

The Acknowledge–Link–Let Go (ALL) process helps you to become aware of your glasses and to see the world around you more objectively. Once you understand your core beliefs they can provide a powerful link in the ALL process. When you have insight into your most important links and accept that your emotions make perfect sense given what you have gone through, it is a lot easier to let go of them. As you continue to practise the ALL technique, your core beliefs and self-talk become less rigid, which gives you greater awareness and control of your feelings. Your internal world becomes safer and you can move from beating yourself up to backing yourself up.

Here are some examples of how ALL links with core beliefs.

Hello feeling like nobody likes me.
It makes perfect sense that you are here because I grew up feeling like a burden to my parents.
Take a deep breath, drop your shoulders and let it go.

Hello feeling anxious.
It makes perfect sense that you are here because when I was a child my father was very anxious and always told me the world is a dangerous place and I believed him.
Take a deep breath, drop your shoulders and let it go.

Hello feeling bad about myself.

It makes perfect sense that you are here because when I spoke about what Dad had done he turned on me and looked at me in disgust. I had no choice but to agree with him and see myself as disgusting and bad. It makes perfect sense that I feel this way but it does not make it true.

Take a deep breath, drop your shoulders and let it go.

Mindfulness and thoughts

As soon as you feel judged by someone else or by your own negative self-talk, the automatic response is for the brain to move towards the red zone. Therefore judging yourself with negative self-talk coming from negative core beliefs is a powerful red-brain trigger. Mindfulness trains your mind to see clearly and not get caught up in believing your projections. It reshapes your internal dialogue and self-talk, which leads to increased self-compassion. Then the critical inner voice can begin to be dismantled and a more mindful, kind and caring voice can start to develop.

Many clients and course participants see this as the greatest benefit of learning to practise mindfulness. When you become more compassionate, kinder and less judgmental towards yourself, your internal world becomes a safer place. This leads to you feeling calmer, happier and more in control. Because of this, practising mindfulness can soften and, in time, undo the internal patterns that were created in a negative childhood dynamic.

There will always be events and circumstances in your life that you cannot control. But if you learn to control your thoughts, suddenly your mood and behaviour no longer depend on your circumstances but on *you*. Through practising mindfulness you will become more aware of your thoughts and regain control over them.

INSIGHT INSPIRATION

1. Write down your three most often occurring stressful thoughts — three thoughts that you have on a regular basis that make you feel stressed. For example, *I don't have enough money. I am not a good mother. I don't have enough time. I hate my job.*

1.

2.

3.

2. Finish these sentences with the very first thing that comes to your mind, even if it does not make any sense.

I am

Others are

I have to be   or else

The world is

3. As a child what was your role in the family?

4. Take a moment to look at your answers to the above questions. Are your reoccurring stressful thoughts and your answers to question 2 linked? And how do your stressful thoughts relate to your role in the family as a child?

5. How have these thoughts and beliefs impacted your life?

6. Look at your stressful thoughts and identify which emotion they bring out in you. Then look at your beliefs about yourself and the world (question 2) and your role in the family as a child. Why does this emotion make perfect sense? Use these insights for the ALL process and practise these on a regular basis.

ALL for stressful thought 1.

1. Hello   (emotion)

2. It makes perfect sense that you are here because

3. Breathe out, drop your shoulders and let it go.

ALL for stressful thought 2.

1. Hello   (emotion)

2. It makes perfect sense that you are here because

3. Breathe out, drop your shoulders and let it go.

ALL for stressful thought 3.

1. Hello   (emotion)

2. It makes perfect sense that you are here because

3. Breathe out, drop your shoulders and let it go.

Chapter 6:
CHANGING STRESSFUL THOUGHTS

When you begin to practise mindfulness, you will recognize your reoccurring stressful thoughts and become more aware of how quickly they make your red brain kick into gear. The next logical question is: how do I change my stressful thoughts?

General mindfulness practice retrains your brain, and it retrains your thinking to be kinder and less judgmental. This will lead to an overall reduction of stressful thoughts. However, we each have deeply rooted specific stressful thoughts that are hard to get rid of. It can be very useful, besides your regular mindfulness practice, to pay some extra attention to these thoughts and work on changing them into more helpful thoughts. There are several ways in which you can do this. In my experience the self-inquiry technique by Byron Katie is one of the most effective ways of changing persistent, stressful or negative thoughts.

Byron Katie's approach has deeply impacted my mindfulness practice. In her book *Loving What Is*, she describes how in 1986, at the bottom of a ten-year spiral into depression, rage and self-loathing, she woke up one morning to a state of constant joy that has never left her. She realized that when she believed her stressful thoughts, she suffered, but that when she questioned them, she didn't suffer, and that this is true for every human being. Her simple yet powerful process of inquiry is called The Work (www.thework.com).

Byron Katie's self-inquiry technique gently forces you to take a step back and look at your stressful thoughts from a different perspective. Then you cannot help but start seeing things differently. When you become unstuck from your stressful thoughts, you find out that they are indeed just thoughts. Thoughts that make perfect sense given what you have gone through. Thoughts that *feel* very true but *are not* necessarily true.

Identifying your stressful thoughts

According to the CBT model, an event that triggers a stressful thought leads to feelings of stress and a red-brain reaction, which often has negative consequences. In order to change this sequence you first need to identify the thought that is triggering the stress. It is not always easy to identify your thoughts, but you can recognize when you are becoming stressed. You may notice your shoulders becoming tense, your breathing becoming shallow and your heart starting to beat faster. Most people describe it as a feeling of pressure and restriction on their chest, in their head or stomach. One way of identifying your stressful thoughts is to pause when you have these feelings and focus on your thoughts in that moment. Another way to identify your stressful thoughts is to think about a situation that makes you feel stressed or an unpleasant emotion, then bring your awareness to your thoughts.

Your thoughts consist of many layers. The top layers are often nicely constructed and are a lot more reasonable then the lower layers. The closer to the underlying, raw and 'ugly' thought, the more effect the technique will have. Here is an example:

Top-layer thought: *I am not sure if I can retire comfortably.*
No one can be really sure of this but it won't be stressful for everyone. This means that the stress will come from an underlying thought or fear, which could be:
I need to be sure I can retire comfortably, or
I won't be able to retire comfortably.

You can go one layer deeper by asking yourself, 'And what would happen then? What am I really afraid of?' For example:
If I can't retire comfortably, I will end up alone.
If I can't retire comfortably, I will end up homeless.
If I can't retire comfortably, I will become unhappy.

Another useful question to ask yourself is: 'If I can't retire comfortably, what would that say about me?' For example:
If I can't retire comfortably, it means that I have failed.
If I can't retire comfortably, it means I will become a burden to others and they will resent me for it.

One way to determine whether a particular thought is appropriate to use for the self-inquiry technique is to note your immediate physical response when you think or say the thought out loud. If you get an immediate unpleasant emotional or physical response you have likely found a core stressful thought. When you have identified a thought that causes you stress you can apply the following steps of Byron Katie's self-inquiry process, called The Work.

ASK THE QUESTIONS

1. Is it true?

This first question can only be answered with a 'yes' or 'no'; 'maybe' is not allowed. When you ask yourself the question, you will immediately look at your thought in a more rational way and you will find that very often the answer is *No, that thought is actually not true*. When you realize this, your perspective changes and you begin to become unstuck from the stressful thought. Other times the answer will be *Yes, that thought is true*. Regardless of whether your stressful thought is true or not, you simply answer the question and then move on to the next question.

2. Can I absolutely know that it is true?

Again this question can only be answered with a 'yes' or a 'no'. Often you will find that the answer is no because most of the time you cannot be 100 per cent sure that something is true or will happen. When your answer is no, the awareness comes in that this thought that *feels* so true actually is not true. This creates space for further enquiry. Other times the answer may be *Yes, I can absolutely know that this thought is true.* Regardless of whether the answer is yes or no, you simply answer the question and then move on to the next question.

3. How do I react, what happens, when I believe that thought?

You can comment on how believing this thought makes you feel, how it makes you want to react and how that affects your health, happiness and relationships or perhaps work performance. For example:

When I believe the thought, 'I will lose my job if I don't perform better,' it makes me feel stressed and worried, which makes it even harder to do my job well.

When I believe the thought, 'I am ugly', I become filled with self-hatred. I then respond by binge eating and feel guilty afterwards.

Regardless of your response, by answering this question you will probably find that believing your stressful thoughts makes you feel bad and respond in ways you don't like. If you have a positive response to this question, then there is no need to use the self-inquiry process on that thought. Most people are only motivated to change thoughts that don't work for them. Feel free to keep the ones that work for you.

4. Who would I be without the thought?

If tomorrow morning you wake up and the thought is gone, completely erased from your mind, what would be different about you? What would be different about the way you feel and react and how would that change your situation? Often people respond to this question by saying, 'I would be so much lighter and more relaxed,' or 'I would be less worried and better able to do my job,' or 'I would actually enjoy my life a lot more.' Whatever your answer is, envision it and let it sink in.

TURN IT AROUND

The last and perhaps most important step is the turn-around. I encourage you to see it as a thought experiment, a way to try out different thoughts to see how they work for you.

A statement can be turned around to the self, to the other, and to the opposite. For example, *Mike should understand me* turns around to:

- Mike shouldn't understand me. (to the opposite)
- I should understand me. (to the self)
- I should understand Mike. (to the other)

I don't ever want to experience an argument with Mike again turns around to:

■ I am willing to experience an argument with Mike again.
■ I look forward to experiencing an argument with Mike again.

After you have come up with a turn-around, you then come up with at least three examples of why that turn-around *is* true. It is these examples that really shift your perspective and give you insights. The examples you come up with are the pieces of evidence that your brain needs to truly become unstuck from the stressful thought and begin to believe and strengthen more helpful thoughts.

For example, *Mike should understand me* turns around to:
■ *Mike shouldn't understand me,* or
■ *Mike does not have to understand me.*

Example of why that is true: No one *has* to understand me. Whether someone does or doesn't is up to them. I cannot make him understand me just because I would like him to understand me. He does not *have* to do anything.

Practising the self-inquiry technique will teach you that no one *has* to do anything and it is very stressful to believe that they do. When you believe someone *has* to do something, you are interfering with their personal responsibility, when actually the only thing you can control is what *you* do. Therefore, it is a way of thinking that could easily lead to stress. Of course, you would prefer it if people did things a certain way, but that is not the same thing as believing they *should* do things a certain way.

The release that comes from realizing that other people don't have to do anything and you can control only your own life gives so much freedom. This does not mean that you no longer share with others your opinion or requests, but you leave with them the responsibility of what they do with that. It is their business; what you do and how you respond to them is your business. Even when the person you are talking to is your partner or grown-up child, ultimately they are responsible for their actions. This opens up the way to genuine conversation and enquiry of their reasons behind what they do.

> *'The what-ifs and should-haves will eat your brain.'*
> — JOHN O'CALLAGHAN

Mike should understand me turns around to *I should understand me.*

Here is an example of why this is true.

I am so focused on Mike's behaviour that I lose sight of understanding my own thoughts and feelings and what it is I really need to focus on. If I don't understand myself and know what it really is that I want, how can Mike understand me?

Mike should understand me turns around to *I should understand Mike.*

Here is an example of why this is true.

I have been so focused on him not understanding me that I haven't taken the time to try to understand him. Which is not fair.

I don't ever want to experience an argument with Mike again turns around to *I am willing to experience an argument with Mike again.* Here is an example of why this is true.

Experiencing another argument with Mike will only make me stronger and teach me valuable lessons.

I don't ever want to experience an argument with Mike again turns around to *I look forward to experiencing an argument with Mike again.*

Here is an example of why this could be true.

Experiencing another argument with Mike will only make me stronger and teach me valuable lessons. It helps us to see where things are going wrong and what we should change to make it better. Arguments are not fun but in the end we always work through them and it brings us closer together.

I have used this technique many times and it has truly reshaped some of my persistent, negative and stressful thoughts. One of my most stressful thoughts used to be, 'I don't have enough time.' I used to have this thought several times a day, and every time I would feel stressed and irritated. My shoulders would become tense, my breathing would become shallow, and my heart rate would increase. The red brain would be activated swiftly and lead to tunnel vision and losing sight of the bigger picture.

My thinking became black-and-white and judgmental. This led to irritation towards the people around me, but mostly with myself.

Then I started to apply Byron Katie's self-inquiry technique to this stressful thought: 'I cannot be late.'

1. Is it true?
I cannot be late — is that true? The answer is no, because it is possible that I can be late.

2. Can I absolutely know that it is true?
No, I can't.

3. How do I react, what happens, when I believe that thought?
I feel stressed, tense and irritated. It makes me angry with myself and others. It makes me disorganized and forgetful and it creates more negative thoughts.

4. Who would I be without the thought?
Without the thought I would be much more relaxed and more patient with myself. I would probably find it easier to get more organized and plan my mornings differently so I won't be as late the next time!

5. Turn the thought around:
I *can* be late.
Why is that true?

It is a fact that I can be late. I don't like being late, but it *is* possible and it won't be the end of the world. In fact, probably no one at work will notice and if they do it really doesn't matter. I have been late before and it has never been an issue, I just make up the time by working longer. Wow, it is really not such a big deal at all!

Even though this exercise helped me to stress less about being late it did not have the eye-opening and calming effect I knew was possible. So, I looked at the situation again and tried to use Acknowledge–Link–Let Go in the moments I felt stressed. This made me aware of the following underlying thoughts:

■ I don't have enough time.
■ I am not supported.
■ I might fail to do what is expected of me.

Then I thought about my role in the family as a child and replied to these thoughts by saying, 'It makes perfect sense you are here given what I have gone through.' I became aware that growing up I experienced my family and environment as one where there was never enough. There was not enough money, there was not enough time, not enough resources. I am the oldest child, I needed to be responsible and always do my best at everything. Looking back I realized that I experienced this as having the burden of expectation and responsibility combined with a lack of resources and support. So, my thoughts made perfect sense! And they *felt* so true because they were true when I was a child.

Doing the self-inquiry technique again, with these insights, made it easier for me to start with the right thoughts, the thoughts that were really causing the stress. 'I don't have enough time.'

1. Is it true?

I don't have enough time — is that true? My first response in the moment is 'yes' it is true.

2. Can I absolutely know that it is true?

No I can't. Because what is enough time?

3. How do I react, what happens, when I think that thought?

I feel stressed, tensed and irritated. I become frustrated with myself and it makes me disorganized and forgetful, which leads to more negative thoughts.

4. Who would I be without the thought?

Without the thought I would be more relaxed and more compassionate towards myself. This would make my mornings enjoyable and fun and I would probably find it easier to be organized and plan my mornings differently.

5. Turn the thought around:

I *do* have enough time. Actually I have plenty of time!
Why is that true?
I have plenty of time because each of my days has twenty-four hours. If I arrive an hour late at work I will not have lost that hour, I will just have used it for something else. Even if I sleep in I haven't

lost that time, I have used it to sleep. I can never lose time when I stay in the green-brain state, because in this state I am aware, present, kind and connected. No catastrophe will happen if some things take more time, it will be fine. I can manage it.

Here is an example of another turn-around:

1. Time does not have enough me.
Why is that true?
When I am stressed, irritated and impatient I am not aware, present and connected. I am unmindful and then it is true that my time does not have enough me. Every time I'm in the red-brain state the best part of me checks out and then my time does not have enough me.

This is when I got the wow, that is really true, moment. I only lose resources when I go into the red brain. Not because I am losing time but because I 'lose' the green-brain version of myself! This makes perfect sense!

Because the thoughts 'I can't be late' and 'I don't have enough time' had been used so often they were strong and dominant pathways in my brain. My new insight alone did not erase those pathways, so the thoughts continued to pop up for some time. But now I did not have to believe the thought. I could greet it with kindness and then quickly ask myself, is that true? And then turn it around to *I have plenty of time* or *My time needs more of me*, which in time became my mantra in the form of 'Be here now'.

Because I kept reminding myself that I have plenty of time I became much more relaxed and better able to plan and organize (it is so much easier in a green-brain state!). This literally resulted in me having more time. Whatever you do, you always do it better from a green brain, so identifying the thoughts that activate the red brain and replacing them with thoughts that activate the green brain will make you more effective. The consequence is a calmer, kinder and happier you.

What if it doesn't work?

FINDING THE RIGHT STRESSFUL THOUGHT

It often takes some introspection and trying the technique on different thoughts before you get to the real stressful thought. Just as in my example, you might start with a thought that is actually not at the core of the stress. Check in with yourself when you are feeling stressed, anxious or down, and monitor your thoughts without filtering them. What is the raw, unfiltered thought that creates a strong response in your body or emotions? That will often be the one you need to use for self-inquiry. Don't worry if you are struggling to find that core thought — this is work in progress. Just keep going, keep trying different thoughts until you find the one that really stands out.

FINDING THE RIGHT NEW THOUGHT

Feel free to play around with alternative thoughts. The direct turn-around is often just a starting point, and something will come up that really clicks with you. For example, my direct turn-around was 'I have enough time' but I then changed it into 'I have plenty of time.' 'Plenty' feels more abundant then 'enough' and therefore it is a stronger antidote to my core beliefs of there not being enough. Try out different ones until you find something that really clicks with you and gives you that feeling of relief.

RESULT COMES WITH PRACTICE

It takes time and practice to change those stress-based pathways in your brain. Every time you practise this technique you are building and strengthening more helpful thoughts. It is useful to go through all the steps at least once, and I recommend that you write each step and your answer down. Beginning to practise the helpful thought takes conscious effort. The aim is to stick with it and *fake it till you make it*. In time these new and helpful thoughts will become your new automatic thoughts.

EXERCISE 6:
CHANGING STRESSFUL THOUGHTS

Use this technique on your reoccurring stressful thoughts.

Step 1. Reoccuring stressful thought one.

1. Is it true? Yes or no?

2. Can you absolutely know that it is true? Yes or no?

3. How do you react, what happens, when you think that thought? What happens when you believe that thought? How do you feel? What does it make you want to do?

4. Who would you be without the thought? If tomorrow when you wake up, everything is the same but this thought has been erased from your mind, what would be different about you?

5. Turn the thought around.

Turn-around one.

Give three examples why that is true.

1.

2.

3.

Can you find another turn-around?
Turn-around two.

Give three examples why that is true.
1.

2.

3.

Can you find another turn-around?
Turn-around three.

Give three examples why that is true.
1.

2.

3.

Step 2. Reoccuring stressful thought two.
1. Is it true? Yes or no?

2. Can you absolutely know that it is true? Yes or no?

3. How do you react when you think that thought? What happens when you believe that thought? How do you feel? What does it make you want to do?

4. Who would you be without the thought? If tomorrow when you wake up, everything is the same but this thought has been erased from your mind, what would be different about you?

5. Turn the thought around.

Turn-around one.

Give three examples why that is true.
1.
2.
3.

Can you find another turn-around?
Turn-around two.

Give three examples why that is true.
1.
2.
3.

Can you find another turn-around?
Turn-around three.

Give three examples why that is true.
1.
2.
3.

Step 3. Reoccurring stressful thought three.

1. Is it true? Yes or no?

2. Can you absolutely know that it is true? Yes or no?

3. How do you react when you think that thought? What happens when you believe that thought? How do you feel? What does it make you want to do?

4. Who would you be without the thought? If tomorrow when you wake up, everything is the same but this thought has been erased from your mind, what would be different about you?

5. Turn the thought around.

Turn-around one.

Give three examples why that is true.

1.

2.

3.

Can you find another turn-around?

Turn-around two.

Give three examples why that is true.

1.

2.

3.

Can you find another turn-around?

Turn-around three.

Give three examples why that is true.

1.

2.

3.

Chapter 7:
MANTRA

It is likely that you are addicted to thinking. You think all day long; even when you have a moment of peace and quiet you will think of something to think of. It just never stops!

Your thoughts can be positive, neutral or negative. Negative thoughts push your brain towards the red part of the spectrum. When this happens everything that is not a priority for survival is put on hold. This includes learning, the development of skills and building of resources. When in the red zone, your brain's first priority is to make it through that moment.

Positive or neutral thoughts have the opposite effect: they activate the green brain. This makes you more flexible, creative, better at problem-solving and more connected to the people around you. People with more positive thoughts are not only happier, they tend to have more success in life because their brain is better wired to build skills and utilize resources, which makes them better at what they do.

Self-fulfilling prophecy

Positive thoughts have such an impact because they can become self-fulfilling prophecies. Sociologist Robert K Merton first formalized this concept in 1948, describing it thus:

The self-fulfilling prophecy is, in the beginning, a false definition of the situation evoking a new behaviour, which makes the originally false conception come true.

When you believe something negative to be true, you increase the likelihood for it to indeed come true because you are adjusting your brain activity and behaviour to meet your expectation. Remember that your brain does not react to how situations *are* but to how you *perceive* them to be. When you perceive a situation to be negative, the red brain kicks in, your attention narrows and your brain begins to scan the environment looking for evidence that the perceived threat is indeed true. Your thoughts also influence your interpretation of what is happening around you, so it won't be long before you find your 'evidence' and can say to yourself, 'See, I knew this would happen.'

An example of a self-fulfilling prophecy is a fascinating experiment done by a brand of beauty products. In this experiment, two large signs were put above two identical, side-by-side doors. One sign said 'Beautiful' and the other sign said 'Average'. Women who wanted to enter the building had to enter through one of the two doors and they were unaware they were being filmed. It was interesting to see how many of these women chose the 'Average' door, but what was even more interesting to see was what it did to their beauty in that moment. The women who walked through the 'Average' door seemed more rushed, looked down and appeared closed off. The women who walked through the 'Beautiful' door walked slowly, with their heads up and often with a smile on their face. They looked confident, happy and open to connection. The women who believed, in that moment, that they were beautiful, became more beautiful because their posture and facial expression allowed their beauty to show. Nothing is more beautiful than a confident woman who is smiling.

One piece of advice you can take from the self-fulfilling prophecy concept is to never think or say anything about yourself that you don't want to come true. When you say things like, 'I am such a bad cook,' or 'My dog never listens to me,' or 'This is hard work,' or 'My partner does not love me enough,' it will change your brain state and response to the situation, making it truer then it was before you had the thought.

For example, if you think you are not a very good cook while you are cooking dinner it's more likely that you will make mistakes, become distracted and you will focus your attention on the things that go wrong rather than all the things that you do right. If you make a mistake your brain will say, *'See, I knew I am not good at this!'* This will colour your experience of the dinner and you will probably serve the food to your guests with an apology of some kind.

If, however, your thought was, 'I'm going to cook a nice meal,' or 'I'm a good cook,' your experience would be very different. If anything went wrong, you would not think it was a big deal and you would just fix it. You would not serve your meal while making apologies to your guests and they would not even notice little mistakes that you might have made.

Mental stress

Another relevant psychological concept is cognitive dissonance, also known as mental stress. First formalized by Leon Festinger, it focuses on the ways humans always seek internal consistency. When you believe A, you will act according to A and look for evidence of A. When faced with evidence of B instead, internal mental stress is the result. Your brain always seeks to eliminate mental stress so it will either ignore the evidence for B or, if the evidence is strong enough, it will change its belief from A to B to confirm the thought to the reality and therefore eliminate the mental stress.

Ignore the Evidence

Change Your Belief

For example, when you believe that others find you uninteresting, you will register every silence, every eye gaze and the number of times the person you are talking to looks away or checks their phone. You will analyze these neutral events and convince yourself they are evidence of your belief that you are uninteresting. The thought 'I am uninteresting' will make you feel tense and self-conscious, which in turn could make you quiet and withdrawn. Thus your thought has shaped the reality, because silent and withdrawn people are rarely very interesting.

Thoughts become things

Understanding the powerful dynamics of the self-fulfilling prophecy and mental stress can make them tools you can use to your benefit. If thinking negative thoughts pushes your brain towards the red end of the spectrum, causing you to feel negative feelings and giving you negative outcomes, the opposite will happen if you think positive thoughts.

If you think positive thoughts, your brain activity will move towards the green end of the spectrum, making you feel more optimistic and creating more positive outcomes. Remember, your thoughts are the most powerful tool you have in reshaping your brain and reshaping your happiness.

Mindful thinking versus positive thinking

Mindfulness is staying in the moment and connecting with that moment, as it is, in a neutral and kind way. Positive thinking is creating positive expectations that shape your outcomes and your reality. They are complementary approaches that work in different ways.

This is a simplification of a complex reality, but it can be a useful tool in understanding the power of thoughts. In a table it looks like this:

Negative thoughts	Mindfulness	Positive thoughts
Negative beliefs	Neutral beliefs	Positive beliefs
Red brain	Orange/ green brain	Green brain
Negative feelings	Neutral/positive feelings	Positive feelings
Looking for evidence that the negative belief is true	Observing the facts	Looking for evidence that the positive belief is true
Negative behaviours	Neutral/positive behaviours	Neutral/positive behaviours
Negative outcomes	Neutral/positive outcomes	Neutral/positive outcomes
Negative belief is confirmed	Neutral belief is confirmed or a positive surprise	Positive belief is confirmed

Imagine you wake up in the morning. You are still in bed, still sleepy and you realize you have a big day ahead of you. Today is the day you will present your ideas to the rest of your team and they will give you feedback. Then one of these three thoughts pops into your mind: *Today is going to be dreadful,* or *Today will be okay,* or *Today is going to be great!* This is how these three thoughts could influence you and your day.

Thought	Today is going to be dreadful	Today will be okay	Today is going to be great!
Brain state	Red brain	Orange/green brain	Green brain
Feeling	You feel stressed, down and agitated	You feel nervous	You feel confident and positive
Perception (glasses)	You interpret events negatively	You interpret events neutrally	You interpret events positively
Behaviour	You are withdrawn and cranky	You are focused but able to connect	You are open, receptive and chatty
Consequences short-term	People avoid you, you make mistakes and feel unsupported	People are neutral but open towards you, you perform well and feel connected	People are drawn to you, you perform well and feel connected and supported
Outcome	It has become a dreadful day	It has become an okay/good day	It has become a great day

Most people have negative thinking habits, and to jump to positive thinking habits can feel inauthentic. The risk associated with taking such a big step is that the new thoughts won't last. The key for it to work is to come up with thoughts that feel real and authentic to you.

Mantra

The word mantra comes from Sanskrit and means:

> 'A word or group of words that are believed by someone to have spiritual or psychological power. It is also described as "That which protects the mind".'
> — JAN GONDA

The beauty of an affirmation mantra is that it helps keep you on track with your practice. It is a mental reminder of your goals. You can practise a mantra any time, anywhere, and the more you practise it the more it becomes part of your automatic thoughts. The more you think it, the more it shapes your reality.

For example, if your goal is to eat healthier food, one of the things that can help your mind to stay on track with this goal is to use the mantra, 'I eat healthy food.' If you say this to yourself on a regular basis you are more likely to eat healthier foods. If you use the mantra and continue to eat unhealthy food, the discrepancy between your thoughts and your actions will lead to mental stress and one of two things will happen: you will begin to make healthier food choices or you will stop using the mantra. Both options will eliminate the mental stress. Therefore, if you stick with your mantra and use it on a daily basis you are increasing the likelihood of reaching your goal.

Mindful affirmations

A mantra or mindful affirmation is an effective tool to help train your mind to have more mindful thoughts. An effective way to create a mantra is to first think about your goals: what do you want to achieve today, this week or this year? Then, based on your goals, chose one or more sentences that help you stay on track with your goals.

Here are some examples.

Goal	Mantra
To become more confident.	'Actually, I can!'
To be kinder to your partner.	'Today I want to make my partner feel loved.'
To create more fun times with your kids.	'In this house we have fun!'

To relax more.	'I make time to take care of my mind and my body.'
To clear your to-do list.	'By the end of this week my to-do list will be completed.'
Learning to say no.	'This week I will practise my "no".'

Over the page is a mantra I use regularly. It sets me up for a mindful day and helps me to stay on track with my goal of living mindfully. You can try the entire mantra or just a part that stands out to you.

EXERCISE 7:
MINDFULNESS MANTRA

I am kind and non-judgmental, open, curious and confident. I stop arguing with the facts and I accept what is so I can free my mind to make the changes I want to make.

I eat good food and take good care of my body. I sleep well and take time to rest and have fun. I am aware of my body and I appreciate it and what it does for me.

I choose to be aware and conscious and take time every day to be in the here and now. I choose to be mindful of my emotions and process them instead of suppressing them or becoming stuck in them.

I am aware of my thinking, and that it is not the events but my thoughts that cause me stress. I turn my stressful thoughts around and choose thoughts that are helpful to me.

I let go of things that hold me back, I accept what has happened and I let it go so I can be free.

I am grateful for my life and the people in it. I keep my goals in mind and I go confidently in the direction of my dreams.

On-the-run tip: *Write down your mantra and put it in a place where you see it often, for example a note in your wallet, a post-it on your mirror or a screensaver on your phone. Every time you see it you'll automatically read it and you'll have done another exercise.*

Chapter 8:
THE MIND–BODY CONNECTION

We have already looked at different ways you can change your thoughts to become more mindful and positive, making you happier, healthier and more balanced. In this chapter we will look at simple, practical ways you can adjust your body to achieve that same goal.

Your mind and your body are important parts of your being, of who you are. Some see them as separate elements (the dualistic approach), and others consider the mind and the body to be one and the same thing (monistic approach). Whatever your preferred approach, it is fair to say that the mind and the body are both important. More and more research shows that the mind and the body influence each other significantly and that this pathway is a two-way street.

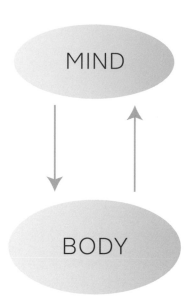

How the mind influences the body

Your mind influences your body and its physical processes. A simple way to experience this is to close your eyes and take as little as thirty seconds to think about a situation that is causing you stress. Do you notice the immediate increase in tension in your muscles, the change in breathing and heart rate? Most people also experience tightness in their chest or their stomach. All of this is a direct result of the release of the stress hormones adrenaline and cortisol. That is how quickly your thoughts change what is happening in your body!

When you are able to control your stressful thoughts and turn them around to helpful thoughts, your body will release stress-reducing hormones, and your muscle tension, heart rate and blood pressure will decrease. Take a moment to close your eyes and think back to a very happy time in your life. See yourself and the people who were there. Do you notice the immediate relaxation in your muscles, your shoulders dropping and your breathing slowing down? Most people will even begin to smile when they recall a happy memory. Just as thinking about a stressful situation quickly increases stress, thinking about a positive situation reduces stress and increases happiness.

How the body influences the mind

Because the mind–body connection is a two-way street, your body also influences your mind. One clear example of this is the significantly increased risk of developing depression or other mood disorders when a physical illness is present. Our physical health and the way we move our body influences the mind. Research by Professor Beilock of the University of Chicago shows that the way we move affects our thoughts, our decisions and even our preferences for particular products. Beilock also found that pacing around a room can enhance creativity, gesturing during a speech can help ensure that you don't draw a blank, kids learn better when their bodies are part of the learning process, walking in nature boosts concentration, and Botox users experience less depression because they cannot frown.

POSTURE

Your body can influence your mind through posture. To experience the significance of how your posture affects your mind, sit in a hunched over, curled-up position for one minute. Notice the immediate effect this change in posture has on how you think and feel. Most people immediately begin to feel unsafe, uncomfortable, anxious or nervous. The opposite is also true. When you sit or stand tall, release the tension from your neck and shoulder area and hold your chin up, you will feel safer, more confident and capable.

Your mind is constantly 'reading' your posture and adjusting how it thinks and feels based on the cues it receives. Hunching over, looking towards the floor and making yourself small sends a powerful signal to your brain that you are not feeling safe and confident. The mind picks up on that signal and it activates the orange- or red-brain state, making stress levels go up.

FACIAL EXPRESSIONS

Facial expressions are another powerful tool to change how you think and feel. To experience this, take a pen and put it horizontally between your teeth, forcing a fake smile. This will seem fake and odd but pay attention to how it makes you *feel*. Most people experience an immediate reduction of stress and increase of happiness by smiling.

Even if the smile is not genuine, it will still affect your mood because your mind is constantly 'reading' your face and adjusting how it thinks and feels based on the cues it receives. Your mouth and eyebrows are especially important messengers to the mind. Simply changing your facial expression to represent the mind state you want to achieve — in this case a green-brain, happy state — will lead to a quick and significant shift towards the desired state.

TAKING UP SPACE

In the animal kingdom there is a clear link between taking up space and dominance. This link is part of our DNA too. When we feel powerful in the moment or long term we tend to naturally take up more space by making ourselves bigger: by standing tall, holding our chin up and making our shoulders broad. In challenging moments this will happen by making large gestures and raising our chin even higher. In moments of pride and victory, such as winning a race or a game, the universal response, even in people born blind, is to raise our arms high in the air. This tendency is programmed in our minds and is part of our subconscious way of responding when we feel powerful.

When we feel powerless or unconfident we do the opposite; we make ourselves small by hunching over, crossing our arms and legs and looking down (or at our phone). We avoid taking up space and make ourselves small in order to protect ourselves.

More research

Psychologist Amy Cuddy from the University of Chicago studied the link between posture and confidence levels. She and her colleagues found that, just as they expected, people who feel confident have low levels of cortisol (the stress hormone) and high levels of testosterone (the confidence and dominance hormone).

Confident	Insecure
▼ cortisol (low stress)	▲ cortisol (high stress)
▲ testosterone (high confidence)	▼ testosterone (low confidence)

They combined this knowledge with studies that were done on apes and found that when a less-dominant ape takes over the role of the alpha male, it takes only a few days for him to start both looking and behaving more dominantly. The change of role affects the ape's posture and his behaviour, and most likely his levels of cortisol and testosterone change accordingly.

Amy Cuddy and her team were interested to find out if the same change in role could achieve that result in humans. They did a double-blind study where the participants had to attend a stressful job interview. One group of participants did a two-minute power pose — for example, standing tall with fists resting on the side of the body (the Wonder Woman pose) — before the interview. The other group was told to do a low power pose — for example, sitting hunched over and looking at the floor — for the same amount of time.

The results showed that a two-minute power pose was followed by a 20 per cent increase in testosterone and a 25 per cent decrease in cortisol. A submissive pose led to a 10 per cent decrease in testosterone and 15 per cent increase in cortisol.

People who were asked to do the power pose felt more confident and capable, and their hormone levels reflected this. Even more surprisingly, without exception, the people who performed the power pose were rated by the people conducting the job interview as more capable, more likeable and better suited for the job. This outcome was independent of the participant's skill set and background. It shows that confident participants perform significantly better socially, which can lead to important benefits such as being hired for a job.

A two-minute power pose, however, does not make you a nicer person or improve your skill set. It is more likely that by doing a two-minute power pose you are preventing the red-brain state from kicking in and hijacking your brain. When your brain is in the red zone and you are highly stressed, it is unlikely you will be able to connect well to others and to show them the real and most likeable and capable you. When stress takes over, you simply cannot be your authentic self and others pick up on that. Doing a power pose allows you to stay on top of your stress so you can show them the best version of you and connect with people in a more natural and authentic way.

The mind of the powerful

A person with low levels of cortisol (low stress) and high testosterone levels (high confidence) is in the green- or orange-brain state and feels confident and optimistic. This leads to assertive responses and more risk-taking. This pattern is also found in powerful and effective leaders and can hugely impact your success both at home and at work.

A person with high cortisol levels (high stress) and low testosterone levels (low confidence) is in the red-brain state and feels quickly overwhelmed and stressed. In this state of stress you cannot perform at your best. This subtle but important change can make the difference between a promotion or no promotion, speaking up about injustice or remaining silent, or managing a chaotic household while keeping your cool or yelling at your kids and then regretting your actions.

Mindfulness of the body

You can use this knowledge on the mind–body connection in several ways. The power pose is a great way to quickly boost your confidence levels in the moment. A way to increase overall confidence is to be mindfully aware of your body. Making changes to your posture and facial expression begins with checking in with your body and auditing it on a regular basis. All it takes is a moment of bringing your awareness to your body and how you are holding it. If you notice you are in a low-power pose, simply adjust your posture by taking up more space. Try the following.

- Uncross your legs (also better for circulation).
- Unwrap your arms.
- Sit up straight without straining your upper back.
- Broaden your shoulders.
- Lift your chin.
- Smile ☺.

EXERCISE 8:
BOOSTING CONFIDENCE

To experience a quick and strong boost in confidence, try the power pose by following these steps.

Step 1. Think of something you have to do or want to achieve, something you do not feel very confident about. This can be anything from sorting out your administration, to painting a fence, to making a meal plan or writing an article.

I want to:

Step 2. Score your confidence level regarding this particular goal on a scale of 1 to 10, with 1 being not confident at all and 10 being very confident.

Confidence level:

Step 3. Stand up, set your alarm for two minutes and do a power pose. Lift your hands in the air, hold your chin up and make it a powerful pose full of energy.

Step 4. The power pose is even more effective when at the same time you envision yourself winning or succeeding at something. You could envision yourself accomplishing a particular goal you have in mind or you can think back to past successful experiences.

When your arms get sore, just notice it in a kind and non-judgmental way and turn your attention back to that image of you winning or succeeding. Try to keep the pose strong and energetic until the two minutes are up.

Step 5. Now think back to the task or goal you rated before you did the pose, and rate your level of confidence again. How confident do you feel now about accomplishing this task or reaching this goal?

Confidence level:

Most people will experience an increase of 2–5 points on their confidence scale, which is pretty amazing considering the fact that this exercise takes only two minutes.

How to apply the power pose in daily life

The power pose is a perfect confidence booster when you are about to go into a challenging situation such as a job interview, a difficult meeting or when going shopping with children. Whenever you are about to do something, and you cannot afford to let stress take over, this is a quick and helpful tool that will give you a boost in confidence. However, the peak in confidence only lasts for 15 to 30 minutes. Therefore, I recommend combining regular practice of the power pose with practising general mindfulness of your posture and facial expression. By combining the two you will have the benefits of the quick peaks of confidence that the power pose gives as well as the overall increase in confidence that comes from a good and open posture. In time you will establish a new base rate of confidence and it won't require any conscious attention.

For example, one of the course participants listened to this explanation of how posture affects the mind and she replied by saying, 'This is true, I did this!' She shared with the group how she was anxious and suicidal at the age of sixteen. Then she decided she had to do something. She decided to start faking being confident. She observed confident people and copied their posture, their way of moving and talking. This felt very inauthentic but according to her anything was better than how she was feeling. After a couple of months she was no longer suicidal and her extreme insecurity had gone. She had become more confident. She faked being confident until she had become it.

 On-the-run tip: *A good, confident posture and a smile is my number-one technique to keep stress under control and deliver a good performance or presentation.*

Chapter 9:
MINDFULNESS FOR CREATING HAPPINESS AND SUCCESS

There are various myths that focus on productivity and happiness, believed by many and helpful to few. Let's explore the truth about the most common of these myths.

The happiness myth

The happiness myth is the idea that being mindful equals being calm and happy *always*. Living mindfully, however, does not mean that you are happy or content all the time, nor does it mean striving to reach a state of constant bliss and happiness. Life would be pretty flat and boring if it were void of any stirring emotions. The more green-brain activity, the more happiness you will have in your life, but there will still be moments of sadness, fear and even anger. The big difference is that these moments are no longer unbearable. They have become manageable and you can see the value of any event and emotion. You have become comfortable riding the waves of emotions caused by life, because you have become a skilled surfer.

Living mindfully means that you aim to be present with whatever happens. You observe the event, thought or emotion in a kind and non-judgmental way, which will activate your green brain. You can still feel sad, frustrated or insecure, but when you are in the green zone these feelings are not overwhelming and you remain in the driver's seat. There is a sense of calm and control and you are responsive instead of reactive. It could mean the difference between yelling at your partner for doing something wrong or explaining to them how important something is to you. It can be the difference between creating even more resistance in a difficult staff member or getting them back on track. It could be the difference between a stress-induced heart attack at age sixty or a long and happy life well into your nineties.

The productivity myth

The productivity myth is another common myth, especially in the corporate world. Many people believe you need stress in order to be motivated and to get work done. They think stress and achievements go hand in hand. It is a myth because stress activates the red brain, which makes it more difficult to achieve your goals (unless your goal is to fight a bear or run from a fire). So, stress and especially stressful thoughts are not as helpful to you as you might think.

You could think of stress as a pimp, someone who has lured people into believing that he is needed for them to be able to be successful and make a profit. Yes, you can be productive and successful with stress as your sidekick and it sometimes might help to achieve things that seemed impossible, but there is a high price to pay. Living with stress is like living with an abusive pimp who teaches you bad habits that damage your health and take away a large chunk of your productivity and your happiness. It is so freeing to realize you do not need stress anymore, you never needed it in the first place. You can be highly successful without being stressed.

> *When you stress less, you achieve more.*

Present-moment awareness

You don't realize how much time you are wasting until you become aware of the present moment. Because of the way our society works — education, work structures, internet, phones, entertainment, advertising — a state of non-presence has become normal. Most of the time we are distracted and think about the next thing instead of what is happening right now and we have come to believe that this is a good thing. In turn, we have also come to believe that as soon as we slow down we are slacking off and will miss out on important things.

Most people seem to be constantly looking for something that will transport them into happiness. Happiness that they believe is in the future. When you tie your happiness to a future goal you believe you cannot be fully satisfied until that goal is accomplished. Physically you are living in the now but your mind is occupied with the future. Your mind is in a state of waiting until 'your happiness' arrives. In reality you are *postponing* your happiness and are not able to see and enjoy all the wonderful things that are happening in the now. Then at some point, you reach your goal and feel a sense of achievement, happiness and relief. This feeling lasts for some time but soon you will find yourself tying your happiness to yet another goal.

'I'm so happy with our new kitchen, isn't it amazing? But we really need to do something about the living room. Once the living room is done I'll be so happy.' (Of course there will be another renovation job to be done after that.)

'I made it through this week of deadlines, what a relief! But the next project really needs to start soon. When that is done I can finally have some down time.' (Of course there will be another important project waiting.)

'When we have an income of $100,000 a year we will be comfortable and life will be great. (Of course by the time you have reached the milestone of earning $100,000 a year you will have adjusted your lifestyle and you will need $150,000 a year to be 'comfortable'.)

As Eckhart Tolle points out:

> *'The future always comes as the now, therefore if you cannot be happy in the now you will never be happy.'*

For many people it feels wrong to be present in the now and fully enjoy it, as if being present and content should be a reward for hard work and achievements. There is a belief that the contentment should not last too long or you will become lazy. With this mindset, happiness does not come from life, it comes from achievements and you believe that if you allow yourself too much happiness you will not move forward in life.

The truth is that you are reducing your productivity by not allowing yourself to be present in the now. By always striving for the next thing you are damaging your brain, your body, your relationships and your success. Your motivation does not depend on your stress and if it does you should wonder if you are chasing a goal that is worth chasing. When you are not present, when you allow your mind to constantly wander off into the future and focus on the things that you will gain there, you lose sight of all the wonderful moments and things that are happening all around you. Who knows what will happen in the future? All you have is the now. When your mind is occupied with the future you are living in a world that does not exist yet and you cannot enjoy or function to your full potential in the now.

Just imagine how freeing it would be to stop believing that you need future goals and achievements to complete your happiness. To believe that you are exactly where you need to be in life.

INSIGHT INSPIRATION

1. To what future goal/achievement are you tying your happiness?

2. If everything else stayed the same but you allowed yourself to be fully present and happy in the now, what would be different?

3. What would you do differently?

4. How would that make you feel?

Gratitude

An effective and fun way to increase present-moment happiness is by practising gratitude. Practising gratitude is nothing more then redirecting your focus from possible good things of the future to the good things of the now.

You can practise gratitude any time and anywhere, but for your initial practice I recommend dedicating a specific moment of your day. You can simply think about the things you are grateful for, but writing them down will increase the impact of the exercise. Sharing with your partner, a friend or your children what you are grateful for is a great way to increase mindful connection.

EXERCISE 9:
GRATITUDE

Step 1. Take a moment to think about your life and what you have to be grateful for.

For example: *I am grateful to be alive. I am grateful for my health, for my body that works for me every single day. I am grateful for my mind that allows me to think and be me, I am grateful for . . .*

Step 2. Be grateful for your partner or a close friend.

Picture this person, their whole body or just their face. What is it about them that you love? What things about their personality do you appreciate? What do you like about the way they look? What do they do for you that you can be grateful for? In your mind thank them for being part of your life.

Step 3. Be grateful for a child in your life.

Picture this child, as if they were standing right in front of you. What is it about them that you love? What do you like about how they look? About what they do? How do they make you feel? Then thank them for being part of your life.

Step 4. Be grateful for your family and friends.

Picture them all or one person in particular, envision what they look like and imagine they are right there standing before you. Take a moment to think about specific things about your family as a whole or about a particular family member. What do you like about your family? What does your family do for you that you can be grateful for? How does that make you feel? Then, in your mind, thank them for being part of your life.

Step 5. Is there anyone else in your life that you can be grateful for?

Picture that person, their whole body or just their face. What is it about them that you like? What do they do for you that you can be grateful for? How do they make you feel? And then, thank them for being part of your life and for who they are and what they do for you.

Step 6. What things can you be grateful for? Even if they are not perfect or exactly what you want?

Are you grateful for your house? Can you be grateful for your means of transportation? Can you be grateful for the money you have? For your job or for the opportunity to take time off? What do you have in your life to be grateful for? Picture those things in front of you and express your gratitude for them.

But how do we move forward?

Many people are high achievers and have big dreams and visions for their future. They might have goals such as starting a family, finding an amazing job or building a business. Often they can see the value of present-moment happiness and they have experienced first hand how constantly chasing achievements burns them out. They feel that something is missing but don't trust that present-moment happiness will help them achieve their goals.

Mindfulness activates present-moment happiness and also creative thinking, energized focus, motivation and big dreams and visions. Therefore, mindfulness is not just the starting point of moving forward, it is also the fuel that keeps you going.

The model of Flow proposed by Vishen Lakhiani states there are four states you can be in: a negative spiral, current-reality trap, stress or flow. According to this model, the state you are in depends on two factors: present-moment happiness and future vision.

Your state	Present-moment happiness	Clear goal/ vision
Negative spiral	NO	NO
Current-reality trap	YES	NO
Stress	NO	YES
Flow	YES	YES

NEGATIVE SPIRAL

If you are not happy in the now and are also not working towards a particular goal or vision, you find yourself in a state called 'negative spiral'. You have negative thoughts and feelings and no direction or plan to take you out of this place of negativity. You feel trapped in your situation and believe you lack the resources and skills to change it. This state comes with low levels of self-esteem and energy. Being stuck in a negative spiral can lead to depressive symptoms.

If you are in a negative spiral, not happy in the now and have no goals to work towards, practising mindfulness can feel useless. If you feel this way, remind yourself that research shows that regular mindfulness practice changes the neural pathways in your brain. It might feel like hard work, but regular mindfulness practice is just as effective in reshaping your brain as regular workouts are effective in building physical strength.

One client found herself trapped in a negative spiral. She is a single mother who recovered from a severe drug addiction and was unable to find a job. She had low energy levels, was overweight and believed that there was no point in trying to make any changes because so far all her attempts had failed. Most days she would go back to bed after dropping her son at school and she would eat large amounts of junk food to feel somewhat better, only to feel worse afterwards. Mindfulness practice made her grow in present-moment awareness. Practising gratitude helped her see the many things she had to be grateful for (and all the successful changes she had already made!). She became grateful for the good things in her life such as regaining custody of her son and being drug-free for more than four years. Focusing on these achievements instilled hope that she would be able to convince someone to hire her. She reconnected with her passion for children and was able to convince the head teacher of her son's school to offer her an internship while she began to study to become a certified teacher's assistant. Now she is studying and working part-time in a job that allows her to assist autistic children — and she loves it.

She is a wonderful example of how becoming happier in the now, by focusing on the good things you already have and seeing how you have accomplished them, opens up a world of possibilities. This change made her grow in self-esteem and reconnect with her passion for children, which created a future vision of working as a teacher's assistant. With both present-moment happiness and a future vision in place, she made a plan and executed it successfully.

CURRENT-REALITY TRAP

In the current-reality trap you are happy in the now but you have no goals or vision for the future. This sounds like a fun place to be, and it is — at least in the short term. This is where many people fear they will end up if they were to let go of the belief that happiness comes from achievements. However, research shows that to reach a place of deeper happiness and fulfillment we require achievements and growth. The need for growth is part of the human fabric, which is reflected in the brain. There is a whole set of 'happy chemicals' reserved for that kind of happiness.

The current-reality trap can lead to stalled motivation and growth due to a lack of goals and future vision. This then leads to superficial happiness and is usually not sustainable in the long term. It often goes hand in hand with addictions because they are shortcuts to a yes in the 'Happy in the now' box. But addictions don't create sustainable happiness that leads to achievements and growth.

If you are stuck in the current-reality trap you probably won't see the need for change until the costs of your situation begin to outweigh the benefits. If this happens, remind yourself that regular practice is effective in changing patterns and finding ways that are more fulfilling.

For example, a client who is a nineteen-year-old student would game for hours on end and was really happy when he was doing this. He did not see any problem with gaming for eight hours every day. When his parents divorced and sold the house he was forced to look for a flat He became overwhelmed with social fears and insecurities. Years of gaming had taken its toll on his mental and emotional growth, his social skills and resilience in the face of change. His excessive gaming had him caught in the current-reality trap where he was happy while he was gaming but overcome by stress in the real world.

Through therapy he was able to see that gaming had left him several years behind in his social development. Most of his peers struggled with the same things he was struggling with, but they overcame it years ago. As he saw that his fears made perfect sense, his goal became to overcome his social fears. Together we made a game plan, but this time it was about how to succeed in social situations. His love for games remained but he now also had real goals and a vision for his future. Towards the end of the therapy he found a flat with people who shared his love for gaming. He now has a job in a game shop and spends his weekends socializing without being overcome by social anxiety. He conquered his crippling fears and lives a life that is fulfilling in several ways, not just one.

A STATE OF STRESS

You end up in a state of stress when you are not happy in the now and you have big dreams and goals for the future. In a state of stress, there is a pressure to move forward to reach these goals, which you believe will make you happy, yet there is no happiness to fuel the move forward. This is not a problem if it lasts for a short while, but when it occurs often or lasts too long, it will cause damage to your brain and the rest of your body, which eventually can lead to burnout.

In a state of stress you are trying to reach your goals but because you have tied your happiness to these goals you are putting your brain in the red- or the orange-brain state. You are trying to reach your goal with a brain state that blocks creative thinking, problem-solving and flexibility. This makes it so much harder to actually reach your goals and you end up feeling frustrated, drained and disappointed.

If you are in the state of stress and start to practise mindfulness, you might feel uncomfortable and restless because it feels like you are wasting time. However, hold on to the fact that spending only a few minutes per day on activating the ideal brain state for achievement — the green brain — will not only make you feel better, it will make you more effective and efficient. This will save more time than it has cost you.

For example, one client used to live in the state of stress. She had a great life with friends, family, a beautiful house by the beach, a fantastic job and plenty of resources. Yet she felt as if life could not 'start', she could not be happy, until she had a partner. This made her unable to enjoy all the wonderful things she already had. Over time, it made her frustrated and angry and her sole focus became finding a life partner. This took all the relaxation and fun out of socializing, which did not make her very attractive to the men she was dating.

She ended up feeling exhausted and burned out, as if she was living her life running on a treadmill without ever reaching her destination. Her way out of this unhelpful dynamic was to 'step off the treadmill' and learn to appreciate and enjoy life just as it was. In time she began to see that life did not have to be perfect to be good.

A STATE OF FLOW

When you are happy in the now and you also have dreams and visions for the future you are tapping into what researchers call a state of flow. When you are in flow, your present-moment happiness activates the green brain, and then adding clear goals to this makes your efforts directed, efficient and focused. You will not only be happier but also more successful in achieving your goal because you are operating from the ideal brain state: the green brain. You are not letting your happiness depend on your achievements but you use your present-moment happiness to fuel your next achievements. In other words: allowing yourself to be happy in the now, no matter what the now is like, is not just about being happy, it is about being smart and creating the ideal circumstances for improvements to happen.

> *The more you can enjoy and be happy in the now, the better your future will be.*

When we combine the brain states and the model of flow we see
this:

Your state	Present-moment happiness	Brain state	Clear goal/ vision	Likelihood of success
Negative spiral	No		No	Low
Current-reality trap	Yes		No	Low
Stress	No		Yes	Low
Flow	Yes		Yes	High

Flow can be a way of life that is a result of being happy in the now
and having a clear goal or vision for your life; it can also be defined
as a momentary brain state. Psychologist Mihaly Csíkszentmihályi
is a leading researcher when it comes to the momentary state of
flow. He defines this state as:

'The mental state of operation in which
a person performing an activity is fully
immersed in a feeling of energized focus, full
involvement, and enjoyment in the process of
the activity. In essence, flow is characterized
by complete absorption in what one does.'

Flow and the brain

Some interesting things happen in the brain when this momentary state of flow is activated. The activity in the prefrontal cortex, the part of the brain that functions as the central executive or the control room, is temporarily reduced. This part of the brain organizes and filters information in efficient and orderly ways to prevent your system from becoming overwhelmed. Having an active control room allows you to function in everyday life. However, when the activity in the prefrontal cortex is temporarily reduced, the rational and judgmental part of the brain is reduced and the more emotional and primal parts take over. This state resembles the brain activity that occurs when you are daydreaming or are about to fall asleep. In this almost 'hypnotic state' thoughts flow freely and links are made that you were not able to make with your conscious thinking. This state of free-flowing ideas, thoughts and images is at the core of creativity.

The difference between daydreaming and flow is that flow comes with increased focus. It releases a neurochemical cocktail in the brain that allows you to absorb more information. The increased creativity and focus combined make the state of flow the ideal brain state for creative thinking, innovation and problem-solving.

Putting it into practice

There are two important things that contribute to activating the state of flow. The first one is a good balance between the difficulty of the task and your skills: if the task is too easy you might become bored and lose focus; if the task is too difficult you become stressed which also blocks flow.

As Csíkszentmihályi puts it:

> *'Flow happens naturally when a person's skills are fully involved in overcoming a challenge that is just about manageable. If challenges are too low, one gets back to flow by increasing them. If challenges are too great, one can return to the flow state by learning new skills.'*

The second key element of the state of flow is focus. Having a strong focus requires you to be fully present with what you are doing without being distracted by external factors (such as multitasking) or internal factors (such as thoughts and emotions). The stronger the focus you bring to the task, the more likely you are to enter into a state of flow.

The increased creativity and focus that come with the state of flow lead to increased achievements. Knowing this can give you a new approach to productivity. When you get stuck and are in need of creative solutions or ideas, rather than trying harder, pause and activate the state of flow, because in flow the productivity and the ideas will flow easily.

EXERCISE 10:
FLOW

Activating the state of flow is especially useful when you are in need of new ideas or solutions to problems.

Step 1. Think about a situation that is causing you stress. Then finish this sentence with a clear goal for improving the situation and write it down.

How do I . . . . / How can I . . . .

For example: *How do I generate more revenue? How can I keep my toddler calm in the supermarket? How can I make more time to exercise?*

Step 2. Focus on your breath. Notice what it feels like to breathe in and out. Do this without giving your opinion or wanting to change anything. Simply observe your breath and notice what happens in your body as you breathe in and out.

Step 3. When you feel calm, focus on the question or desired outcome you have written down and write down whatever comes to your mind. When doing this make sure your hand keeps moving. Do not stop and think, just write down whatever comes to mind. Allow the thoughts and ideas to flow freely by not interrupting or judging them. When you begin to judge or evaluate your ideas, gently and kindly bring your attention back to your breath and the original question or goal.

Step 4. When you feel as if you are running out of ideas, make yourself continue for at least three more minutes!

Step 5. Once you have enough ideas, put down your pen. Now it is time to use your analyzing skills to see which ideas are useful.

TIP: Coming up with ideas to reach a positive goal is easier for your brain then coming up with ideas to avoid something negative. For example:

How can my partner and I become closer? *works better than* How can we stop arguing?

Keep your goals positive and you will be surprised at the ideas you will come up with.

Overcoming blockages to flow

The most common blockages to entering or remaining in a state of flow are:

■ Trying.

■ Imbalance between skills and challenges.

■ Negative thoughts and feelings.

TRYING

Flow happens in the green-brain state. When you are trying or striving, however, you activate the orange — achieving — brain state. There is nothing wrong with this, but it is not the optimal brain state for creativity. In the brain state of achieving you experience immediate thinking: your brain will scan your memory to look for knowledge and past events that were similar, and come up with ideas that are not new but instead familiar and obvious.

IMBALANCE BETWEEN SKILLS AND CHALLENGES

A good balance between the task and your skills is helpful when it comes to reaching a state of flow. As Csíkszentmihályi describes, a task cannot be too easy, nor should it be too difficult.

If you are struggling to reach a state of flow, think about the diagram below and where you find yourself. Then ask yourself the question: Is there anything I can adjust or change to move closer to the flow channel?

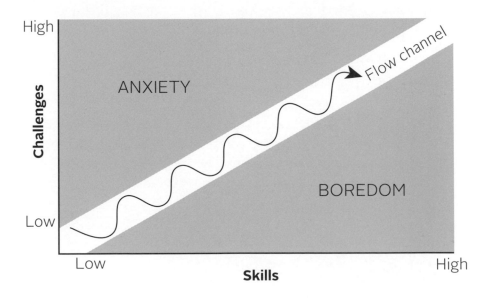

NEGATIVE THOUGHTS AND FEELINGS

Negative thoughts tend to block the state of flow. Not only do they pose a distraction, your negative thoughts trigger the sequence of negative feelings that block flow.

Thoughts like:

I'm/my work is not good enough.

Others will judge me/my work.

I don't have enough time/support/resources/talent.

These thoughts immediately change your position on the flow chart and place you in the anxiety domain. This will, without exception, activate stress. To combat this, use Byron Katie's self-inquiry technique (see page 113) to turn these thoughts around. Or you can use the Acknowledge–Link–Let Go (ALL) model of processing emotions (see page 59) to process the negative emotions. These techniques help bring your brain back to the green brain from where you can reactivate the state of flow.

 On-the-run tip: *When you are working on something and you feel stressed, remind yourself that if you 'take 5' you 'win 50'. In other words, if you take 5 minutes to activate flow, you will save at least 50 minutes on the total time you spend on this task.*

Chapter 10:
THE BEGINNER'S MIND

One of the key elements of mindfulness is the beginner's mind. The beginner's mind is one of openness and curiosity without preconceived ideas and concepts. In a way it is learning to approach and see things like a child again. This may sound strange because our society and educational system is focused on moving us away from the beginner's mind and making us experts in various areas. Being a beginner is not often seen as something valuable but rather as something unworthy and uncomfortable that we need to change.

Mindfulness, however, sees the beginner's mind as a powerful tool, a way to achieve a calm, open and neutral way of thinking. The beginner's mind is also a technique to activate the green-brain state in challenging situations and see the situation from a mindful perspective rather than through your unhelpful glasses (your preconceived ideas and concepts that make you think and feel in a certain way). Approaching a challenging situation with a beginner's mind creates space for intuition, awareness and seeing things in a new light rather than automatically boxing it in.

The beginner's mind technique creates a 'feeling experience' of a situation rather than an intellectual and analytical experience. This is because the beginner's mind changes the activity in your brain from what we call 'top-down processing' to 'bottom-up processing'.

The brain

Your brain is divided into three main areas. The first one is the brain stem. This is where our most basic life functions are located, such as breathing, heart rate and alertness. This part of the brain is often called the reptilian brain because it holds the functions we can also observe in reptiles.

The second area is called the limbic area. Among other things, this part of the brain is responsible for motivation, emotions, the attribution of meaning, memory and attachment.

The third area of the brain is known as the neocortex. This is an integrative area that ties the social, the somatic and the analytical together. The neocortex is the part of the brain that gives us our human qualities; it allows us to plan, analyze, organize, empathize and much more.

The neocortex

The neocortex consists of six layers.

BOTTOM-UP PROCESSING

The neocortex can be activated from the bottom up, starting at layer 6, then moving through layer 5, then 4, etc. This is called bottom-up processing.

When you have an experience for the first time you are more likely to use bottom-up processing. Remember when you drove a car for the first time? It is likely you remember this as being an intense and lively experience of the senses. Or think back to your first time on a plane, your first day at a new school, the first time you went on a date with the person who became your partner. Most people remember these occasions as 'feeling' moments. Even thinking back to them can trigger a sensory and emotional experience. It is likely that these were bottom-up experiences because you were experiencing them for the first time and there was no top-level concept created yet. You came into the situation as a beginner, without a 'cognitive box' to put it in.

This open, sensory, curious, not-knowing-what-will-happen-next way of experiencing things comes with your full attention and creates an intense sense of being present.

TOP-DOWN PROCESSING

Your brain also has the ability to activate the neocortex from the top down, starting at layer 1, then layer 2, then 3, etc. This is called

Neocortex

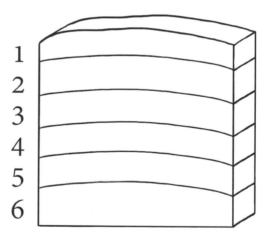

top-down processing. When you have done something repeatedly your mind creates a top-down constraint to understand and store the information. You could say your brain becomes a bit lazy. Instead of taking in everything, your mind ticks the box of what it thinks is happening and goes with that information. This saves the brain energy and is an effective way of processing, leaving more energy and attention for other things.

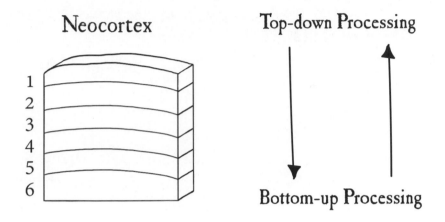

For example, when you now think about driving your car, you probably see it as just another thing you do. It won't trigger an intense 'feeling' experience like it did the very first time you drove your car. After a few months of driving you can drive your car on autopilot. Then only the top levels of the neocortex are activated. This only requires limited attention and focus, because your brain knows what is happening and what to expect.

When you think about your partner after you have been together for a number of years, you are less likely to have the intense experience you had when you first met. Your brain will simply 'activate' the box with this person's name on it and the concept you have constructed.

Box thinking

In most cases the top-down processing system — or box thinking — is very useful. If everything you did or thought about required your full attention and activated a flood of sensory stimuli, you would not get much done. However, doing things on autopilot and simply activating a 'cognitive box' skews the reality. This happens in several ways.

SELECTIVE ATTENTION

One way your brain preserves the cognitive boxes is by selective attention. The mind is looking for information it is expecting to see. In other words, if you expect to see something, it is very likely that you will see that very thing. Your brain looks for 'evidence' that confirms your cognitive box and ignores information that does not fit into the box.

A study by Richard Wiseman, a psychologist from the University of Hertfordshire, showed that people who believed they were generally lucky were more likely to see the £5 note that had been placed on the floor by the researchers. Afterwards the people who believed they were lucky reported thoughts such as 'Wow, lucky me!', which confirmed and reinforced their pre-existing belief. The people who believed they were unlucky mostly stepped over the money without noticing it.

BENDING THE FACTS

Another way the mind conserves its cognitive boxes is by bending the facts. At a subconscious level, the mind reconstructs information to fit into the box. It does this because perceiving information that does not fit the box would require energy-costing processes to create another cognitive box or to change the existing cognitive box. This is an inefficient process that requires full attention and focus. Because the brain is programmed to save energy, it 'makes' the perceived information fit into the existing box.

ATTRIBUTING

The third way in which the mind keeps its cognitive boxes intact is through attributing. When information is perceived that fits the box it will be attributed to the person involved and will be seen as part of their personality. When information is perceived that does not fit the box, the mind attributes it to circumstances or labels it as an exception.

For example, you are convinced your partner does not care about you and you have put them in the 'they do not care enough about me' box. Your mind will seek ways to confirm this as the truth.

1. Selective attention

Whenever you are with them you will be paying attention to everything they do wrong (in your eyes). Your mind will not register the times they are caring and considerate.

2. Bending the facts

When you notice your partner doing something sweet you are likely to dismiss it as unimportant.

3. Attribution

When your partner does something sweet or caring you might think they are doing it for the wrong reasons. Or you will try to make circumstances — rather than your partner — responsible for the positive behaviour.

So, no matter the facts of the situation, your mind tries to keep your cognitive boxes intact, just to prevent having to switch to the energy-consuming bottom-up processing. When the preconceived ideas are positive this does not lead to problems. When the preconceived ideas are negative it leads to negative thoughts and feelings and stress.

The beginner's mind is a way to break free from unhelpful top-down constraints or boxes and make the mind apply bottom-up processing again. When you apply bottom-up processing the traps of selective attention, bending the facts and attribution are dealt with, which will result in a quick reduction of stress plus a new perspective on the situation.

EXERCISE 11:
BEGINNER'S MIND

Step 1. For a moment, pretend you are from the planet Mars. Take an object — something you use in regular life — and observe it in an open, curious and non-judgmental way, as if you have never seen it before. Try to figure out what it is. Notice the colour, the shape, the details. Use your touch and smell to explore and observe the object.

Step 2. Did you notice anything different or new when you were observing the object in this way?

Step 3. Now focus on a situation that causes you stress or triggers a negative emotional response. Apply the beginner's mind to this situation by observing the facts in an open, curious and non-judgmental way, as if you were experiencing it for the first time. It might help if you imagine once again you are from the planet Mars. What do you hear and see? Try to leave your own thoughts and feelings out of the observation. If they pop up, simply notice this and in a kind and non-judgmental way turn your attention back to the situation.

Step 4. What are you becoming aware of now?

How to apply the beginner's mind in daily life

Regular practice of the beginner's mind will make it easier for your brain to access bottom-up processing. Your brain literally strengthens the bottom-up pathways every time you use them.

You can practise the beginner's mind any time, anywhere. An effective way to practise is to use the beginner's mind whenever you are feeling stressed, frustrated or any other negative emotion. You can use it in the moment or afterwards by focusing on the facts of the situation, without engaging your opinions and preconceived ideas. Using the Martian concept can make it easier but it is not necessary. When you apply the beginner's mind in a moment of stress you will find that your stress levels drop, your brain moves towards the green part of the spectrum, which opens up the way to creative thinking, problem-solving and open communication.

When your brain has been hijacked by stress and you have responded in a way that you regret or that just was not effective, it can still pay off to use the beginner's mind. Take a moment to think of the situation and apply the beginner's mind; then, when you are observing the facts of what has happened, you can ask yourself the question: 'How do I want to respond?'

For example, one of my clients works for a large humanitarian aid organization. She had an overloaded work schedule and completely missed the information that on a particular day she was supposed to deliver a speech regarding a new children's project. Normally she would have felt overwhelmed and self-critical, and the stress resulting from her lack of preparation would have hijacked her brain, making her unable to articulate her ideas clearly. She decided to try the beginner's mind. When she looked only at the facts, she saw a room full of people who were all passionate about making this project a success. No one was there to judge her or criticize her; they were all there to make a difference in the lives of underprivileged children. Focusing on these facts, rather than on herself and her lack of preparation, allowed her to move away from the red brain and into the green brain. It reduced her stress and, instead of literally wanting to run away and hide, she became excited about being part of this group of people. She was able to convey her message, and her involvement in the project became a huge success.

When it doesn't work

Like most mindfulness techniques, the hardest part is to make a conscious effort to put it into practice. At some level we like our glasses and our boxes, and letting go of them can seem very unfair and wrong, and sometimes leaves us feeling very vulnerable. Applying the beginner's mind is hardest when you are angry with someone, or a situation has hurt you, but in those situations it can be most effective.

When you are faced with internal resistance, I recommend that you respond in a kind and non-judgmental way. One way to mindfully connect with your resistance is by using Acknowledge–Link–Let Go. Often your resistance will lessen. Hopefully you will begin to see that the only one who is suffering from holding on to this 'box thinking' is you, and that you owe it to yourself to become unstuck from it.

If this process does not happen, don't judge it but continue to meet your resistance with kindness and acceptance. Self-compassion is the fastest way to the green brain.

 On-the-run tip: *Try the beginner's mind when you need new ideas or solutions at work. It helps you think 'out of the box' and come up with new, creative ideas.*

Chapter 11:
MINDFULNESS FOR IMPROVING RELATIONSHIPS

Happiness is a well-studied phenomenon on which countless studies have been conducted. One of the clearest findings to emerge from research on happiness is that we are social creatures. Did you know that not having close relationships poses the same risk to your health as smoking and obesity?

Relationships include romantic relationships, relationships with family members, friends, neighbours, colleagues and anyone we feel connected to. Both the quality and the quantity of our relationships impact our health, longevity and psychological wellbeing. Having a network of social connections or a few close relationships increases immune-system function and helps protect us from cardiovascular disease and age-related mental decline.

Mindful connection

Mindful connection is a bottom-up 'feeling experience' that can occur when two brains in the green brain state interact. Mindful connection can be a deep and rewarding experience, the kind that strengthens our bond and makes us feel loved, supported, understood and valued. It is sometimes described as 'heart to heart' connection.

In mindful connection, the lower levels of the cortex and the subcortical regions of the brain are activated. This is responsible for giving you a 'feeling experience' that your brain interprets as meaningful. Rapid neural signal transfer takes place and the chemical oxytocin (among others) is released, leading to softened facial muscles, tone and an increased openness of the perceptual system.

How to achieve mindful connection

Just like general mindfulness, mindful connection has the following two components.

- Attention — paying attention to both the person we are connecting with and what they are sharing with us.
- Attitude — paying attention in a kind and non-judgmental way.

We can focus our attention in different ways, and *how* we focus our attention determines if the interaction will be mindful or unmindful. Mindfully paying attention means focusing on the person and their message and fighting outward distractions. This sounds simple but in reality it can be very hard. Often we are not actually paying attention when talking to others; instead we are looking at our phone, our laptop, cooking dinner or tidying up. It is possible to listen when you are doing something else, but as soon as you do more than one thing at a time you are multitasking. When you multitask, your brain seeks ways to minimize the energy spent on each task, and activating top-down processing is one of the brain's first go-to ways to preserve energy. As we discussed in the previous chapter, top-down processing causes boxed-in thinking and activation of preconceived ideas and opinions. The more distractions, the more top-down processing and the more difficult it becomes to connect mindfully.

There is a time and place for multitasking, but it is not when you want to mindfully connect with someone. Mindful connection starts with giving your undivided attention to both the person and what they are sharing with you.

> *In order to have mindful connection you need to fight external distractions — disconnect to connect.*

The second element to mindful connection is attitude. In other words, how do you treat the information that is being shared with you? Mindful connection comes from accepting the other person's thoughts and feelings and staying out of judgment. It is listening with the aim to understand, not with the aim to reply. Your opinions and judgments come up automatically and therefore it is hard to not be distracted by them but with practice you can learn to let them go and listen without being distracted by your opinions or thoughts.

> *In order to have mindful connection you need to fight internal distractions — notice them and let go.*

Professor Daniel Siegel sums it up beautifully in his definition of mindful connection or, as he calls it, attunement.

'Attunement is how we focus our attention on others and take their essence into our world.'

INSIGHT INSPIRATION

1. Who are the most important people in your life?

2. What *external* distractions get in the way of mindfully connecting with them (for example, your phone, television or housework)?

3. What *internal* distractions get in the way of mindfully connecting with them (for example, worries about work, tiredness, judgments)?

4. What changes are you willing to make to ensure fewer distractions and more moments of mindful connection with these important people?

 On-the-run tip: *Practise your listening skills by starting a conversation with a question. Try to listen to the answer with the aim of understanding the person and their experience, without adding anything to it.*

Oxytocin

Also known as the 'love hormone' or 'cuddle hormone', oxytocin is not the only chemical responsible for mindful connection but it does play a crucial role in social connection and activation of the green brain. This hormone has many beneficial effects, including the following.

- Increases energy.
- Fights depressive symptoms.
- Promotes social behaviour and bonding.
- Makes us better at picking up and understanding social cues.
- Lowers stress and anxiety (by lowering cortisol and adrenaline levels).
- Makes learning more effective.
- Makes you more trusting.
- Makes you more trustworthy.
- Makes you more generous.

> '*Oxytocin solidifies the glue that binds us into meaningful and important relationships.*'
> **— SARA ALGOE**

Oxytocin plays a key role in mindful connection. The more often your brain produces oxytocin the easier it becomes for the brain to produce it. Oxytocin can't be purchased in a pharmacy, but luckily research shows you can boost your oxytocin levels naturally with the following steps.

1. EYE CONTACT

One of the reasons couples who are in love gaze into each other's eyes is because of high oxytocin levels. Research shows that prolonged eye contact is not only a result of high oxytocin, it can also be a way to raise oxytocin.

Most people avoid looking in another's eyes for a long time; instead they glance over people. You can be around people all day without really making eye contact. To change this, make a conscious effort to look people in the eye. It might feel strange and unnatural in the beginning, but you will feel more connected to others and they will feel more connected to you. There is something open and genuine about having someone really look you in the eye when they are talking to you. It literally makes you feel seen.

2. TOUCH

Touch is another way to naturally raise oxytocin levels. A hug, a handshake, putting your hand on someone's shoulder. People with high oxytocin levels are more likely to touch others but it also works the other way around; making a conscious effort to (appropriately) touch others will increase oxytocin levels in both you and the other person. It will make them feel touched in the positive sense of the word.

Some examples from studies include: when a teacher touches a student gently on their back or shoulder they are more likely to participate in class; athletes who high-five or hug their team-mates perform better in team sport; a touch can make patients like their doctors more; when faced with a stressful situation, participants who were holding hands or being hugged showed lower levels of stress than those who were not.

 On-the-run tip: *Create micro moments of mindful connection with your family by making a conscious effort to make real eye contact and touch them. It will help you be present and make you feel more connected to them.*

3. PHYSICAL EXERCISE

Exercise is healthy in many ways. One surprising benefit of physical exercise is that it raises oxytocin levels. Studies have been conducted on people running, walking outside and playing team sports, and all of these activities are effective in boosting oxytocin.

We all know that exercise is healthy, but not many people know that it also works as a powerful antidepressant. Various studies show that exercise works better than antidepressant medication in preventing relapse. A study by Dr Blumenthal showed that ten months of regular, moderate exercise outperformed a leading antidepressant (Zoloft) in easing depressive symptoms in young adults. Another study found that walking for 20–30 minutes per day reduced depressive symptoms faster than antidepressant medication. In another study, one group of participants was given both antidepressant medication and an exercise program. The results showed that physical exercise was the more effective depression fighter.

 On-the-run tip: *Parking a block away from your destination, taking the stairs instead of the elevator, having walking-meetings — these are all simple ways to increase both your health and your mood.*

4. GIVING

Studies show that artificially increasing oxytocin levels makes people more generous. Again, this also works the other way around: by giving a gift, no matter how small, you are boosting your oxytocin and that of the person who receives the gift.

By giving a friend a cup of tea, buying a colleague lunch, donating to charity, shouting yourself a gift, even by giving way to a stranger you are raising oxytocin levels in yourself and the other person. This creates a micro moment of connection and makes the other person feel valued.

When it comes to oxytocin, a reward does not achieve the same effect as a gift. A gift that is not linked to achievement but is purely to appreciate a person or a moment is the more powerful oxytocin booster. Such a gift makes people feel loved and appreciated for who they are, not for what they do.

5. PETTING A PET

Research shows that petting a pet raises oxytocin levels quickly. People can have incredibly strong bonds with their pets. Oxytocin plays a key role in this bond. Petting a pet has a strong stress-reducing, calming effect on both the person and the pet. Animal-aided therapies are hence very effective in increasing connection, health and wellbeing in patients. It is even linked to improvement in social skills. Studies show that regular interaction with animals is beneficial for children with autism and the elderly who suffer from depression and loneliness.

6. SEX

Sex stimulates the production of oxytocin in both men and women. Again, this relationship works both ways: having high oxytocin levels will make you feel more connected and more interested in having sex, and having sex will make you feel more connected due to the rise in oxytocin.

Sex is an important part of mindful connection with your partner. When life gets busy it is not always easy to maintain a good sex life or even to maintain intimacy and connection with your partner. Often partners become like colleagues who are running a project together called family. Or partners are so caught up in work that they don't make time to connect with each other. For many busy people sex is just not a priority, but not prioritizing sex has consequences, one of which is that it takes away from mindful connection and opens up the way for irritations and disconnection.

It may feel counter-intuitive but prioritizing intimacy including sex, especially when you are not getting along, does make sense. It boosts oxytocin levels and will help you to reconnect.

7. GRATITUDE

Expressing gratitude, whether it is out loud or internal, raises oxytocin levels. In one study, remembering something nice a partner had done made the participants' oxytocin levels rise and made them feel more loving, peaceful and connected to their partner. A similar study, in which participants were asked to remember or share a positive experience, resulted in a similar rise in positive emotions but no rise in oxytocin. There seems to be something specific about gratitude that activates the oxytocin system in the brain. Perhaps it is because gratitude brings awareness to our co-dependence and the importance of our relationships.

EXERCISE 12:
IMPROVING RELATIONSHIPS

Step 1. Think about an important person in your life.

Step 2. See this person in front of you, their whole body or just their face. Picture them, as if they were right there. What is it about them that you love? What things about their personality do you appreciate? What do they do for you that you can be grateful for?

Step 3. Is there anyone else in your life that you can be grateful for? Picture that person. What is it about them that you like? What do they do for you that you can be grateful for?

On-the-run tip: *If there is tension or irritation in your relationship, dedicate yourself to one week of daily practice of this exercise. Take a moment each day to think of something you appreciate about your partner and write this down. You will notice this helps to see your partner in a more positive light, which opens the way to reconnecting.*

Chapter 12: MINDFULNESS IN CONFLICT

Not many things are as stressful as conflict with an important person in your life. Even conflict with someone who is not important to you can cause high levels of stress. From an evolutionary point of view it makes a lot of sense; in ancient times not only our wellbeing but also our survival depended on relationships and our position within a group. Being in conflict could lead to losing the safety of the group, and therefore alarm bells in our brain go off when conflict arises. That uneasy, uncomfortable or stressful feeling that comes with having a conflict is your brain telling you, 'It's not safe!' Yet conflict, especially conflict with those closest to us, is part of life. Everyone encounters conflict at some stage: conflict with your partner, your mother, a friend or conflict with a colleague.

Conflict begins with the activation of the red-brain state in at least one of the people involved.

The red-brain state is activated when a person *perceives* a threat, be it physical, emotional or social. When you feel offended or mistreated the red brain can kick into gear, which leads to several things. Adrenaline is released within seconds and cortisol is released within minutes. The red-brain dynamics have been described in previous chapters but let me refresh your memory with a list of things that occur when your brain is in the red zone.

Physical effects:
- Tunnel vision
- Shallow breathing
- Stopped or slowed digestion
- Increased blood pressure and blood sugar
- Increased heart rate
- Suppressed immune system
- Tensed muscles

Psychological effects:
- Judgmental and black-and-white thinking
- Feeling stressed

■ Narrow or fixed point of view
■ Unkind manner
■ Disconnection from others

In the case of a physical threat, the stress response will help you to survive: it makes you run faster, fight better, stay completely focused, make quick decisions and respond swiftly to fight off the threat. In case of an emotional or social threat however, activation of the red brain is not helpful at all. The red-brain state blocks you from thinking clearly and objectively. It stops you from seeing the bigger picture and the other person's intention. Instead, your mind takes shortcuts and projects your stressful thoughts onto the situation (usually without realizing it). The red brain makes you impulsive and either suppresses emotions or becomes stuck in them. It blocks effective communication, empathy and connection, which can lead to overreaction and conflict.

It is not difficult to see how these psychological effects can quickly lead to responses that are then perceived as a threat by the other person. This will then trigger the red-brain state in them as well. When two brains in the red-brain state interact, the opposite of mindful connection happens — conflict.

Two brains in the red zone are both perceiving their own reality, which is based on their glasses. They quickly lose connection and because their brain feels threatened they will respond with either defence or attack. It is important to keep in mind that this might not always be visible on the outside; emotionally withdrawing or suppressing anger can be a result of conflict too!

Take the following dialogue between a husband and wife, for example. They both start off with a neutral, green-brain state.

Jane comes home from shopping and takes a loaf of bread out of the bag.
Mark: 'We don't need bread. Didn't you check in the cupboard before you went shopping?'
Looking at the facts, this question is neutral. It could even be seen as very useful advice, to check the cupboard before going shopping. However, it could be interpreted in several ways. Let's say Jane experiences it as criticism. She then *perceives* a threat, which activates her red brain.

She feels a knot in her stomach, her heart rate goes up and her breathing becomes shallow. Her thinking becomes judgmental and black-and-white: '*He always does this, he always criticizes me and questions everything I do!*'

Because her mind feels unsafe it responds with: '*He should just mind his own business and stop judging me.*' These thoughts make her feel both sad and angry and she responds by impulsively reacting in an unkind way: *'If you're so perfect, then why don't you do the shopping from now on!'*

This response is interpreted by Mark as rude, angry and unfair. Therefore his brain *perceives* it as an emotional and personal attack, which activates the red brain in him as well.

Mark feels tension in his neck and shoulder area, his heart rate goes up and his breathing becomes shallow. His thinking becomes judgmental and black-and-white. *'No matter what I say I never do it right, she's never satisfied and always finds something to complain about.'* Because his mind feels unsafe and under attack, it responds with defence. *'She should stop being so bloody moody and stop criticizing everything!'* These thoughts make him feel offended and annoyed and he responds impulsively by walking away in angry silence. The consequence is disconnection, no further communication, and both Jane and Mark feel hurt and angry and blame the other person for causing it.

Stressful thoughts and core beliefs

In order to conserve energy in a potentially dangerous situation, the red brain makes you refer back to old patterns — including reoccurring stressful thoughts and negative core beliefs — which are well-rehearsed neural pathways. Your brain then 'projects' these thoughts and core beliefs onto the situation and looks for 'evidence' that this projection is indeed true. To the person in the red-brain state it feels like they are seeing the facts, when in reality they are seeing a projection of their own thoughts and feelings. Most often people simply assume they are seeing the truth and never question what they think they see. This can easily lead to misunderstandings and conflicts. Here is an example.

James

Reoccurring stressful thought: *I will make a mistake.*
Negative core belief: *I am a failure and others will reject me.*
'*Charlotte is giving me a to-do list because she thinks I will be sitting around doing nothing all day. She even calls to check in on what I'm doing. She must think I'm wasting my time and messing up.*'

Charlotte

Reoccurring stressful thought: *Others need me.*
Negative core beliefs: *I need to be caring and supportive in order not to lose people's love.*
'*James is going through a difficult time with the redundancy. He needs my support but I have to finish my work. I have to help him fill his days and be in touch or else he will think that I don't care and am just doing my own thing.*'

It is not hard to see how believing your projection can lead to disconnection and conflict. In the short term it can cause miscommunication and conflict, and in the long term damaged relationships.

Drama Triangle

Two red brains interacting can easily lead to conflict. The Drama Triangle is a helpful tool in understanding the dynamics of conflict and the role you play in it. A psychological and social model of conflict first described by Stephen Karpman in 1968, it describes three common roles people can take on in conflict.

Victim
Helpless, poor me,
self-pity, blaming

Rescuer
Discounts self/own
needs, enabler,
martyr, stressed

Persecutor
Blaming,
finding fault

VICTIM

The main emotions of the victim are those of sadness and fear. The victim is unable to stand up for themselves and tends to avoid confrontation. In conflict the victim feels hurt, helpless and incapable. They then feel sorry for themself and dwell on this feeling without taking appropriate action to change the situation. The victim feels stuck in victimhood and blames their lack of skills or resources on others. This can lead to passive–aggressive behaviour and giving in to unhelpful things. In this role, the victim does not take responsibility for their own feelings or actions.

Common core belief: *I can't do it by myself/There is something wrong with me.*
Mantra: *I need others.*
Underlying need: *To be rescued.*
Underlying goal: *If you take care of me I can be okay.*

For example, Matt always has problems. He suffers from health issues, struggles at work, and finds it difficult to manage all his responsibilities at home and his finances. There is always a problem — so it seems. When solutions are suggested his response is, 'Yes, but . . .' Because of the strong belief that he is incapable, he constantly feels inadequate. This leads to a strong dependency on others and constant worries about potential future problems.

PERSECUTOR

The main emotion of the persecutor is that of frustration/anger (underlying is fear). In conflict, the persecutor finds fault in others and blames others. They feel angry, frustrated and entitled, and use anger and criticism. The persecutor attacks when venting in order to release stress. They have a strong sense of justice. This combined with feeling under attack leads to hurtful behaviours that are then justified by the persecutor. They focus on other people's faults to avoid having to take responsibility and make changes.

Common core belief: *Others are mean/out to get me.*
Mantra: *It's your fault.*
Underlying need: *To be in control.*
Underlying goal: *As long as I am in control you can't hurt me.*

For example, Diana has a strong presence. She can be charming, or defensive and intimidating and lash out verbally. The sharpness of her tongue and the unpredictability of her moods make others feel uncomfortable. When issues arise she always has to be right and will find clever answers and reasons as to why she is. This makes people pull away. When this happens she feels abandoned and confirmed in her belief that people can't be trusted and she can only rely on herself.

RESCUER

The main emotions for the rescuer are anxiety and guilt. In order to avoid feeling anxious or guilty, the rescuer comes to the rescue of others. They discount their own needs and focus on the needs of others. This may seem selfless and altruistic but this behaviour serves a self-centred purpose: to reduce the rescuer's own anxiety and make them feel responsible and good about themself. By their actions they make themself a martyr who feels overstretched and makes unhealthy sacrifices. They do not take responsibility for their own needs and rob others of the responsibility to take care of theirs.

Common core belief: *I am responsible for others.*
Mantra: *I will fix it.*

Underlying need: *To be valued.*
Underlying goal: *If you need me you won't leave me.*

For example, Katie suffers from adrenal fatigue and has spent many years in an unhealthy relationship. For years she believed her partner would change, and even in the face of clear signs that he wouldn't, she kept fixing things for him in the hope things would get better. She is a 'yes' girl and over-commits because she feels it is her responsibility to help others where she can. In her over-committing she is failing to take care of her own health, her wellbeing and that of her three children.

There is usually one role in which we tend to enter the Drama Triangle. This role is also called our 'starting gate' and is tied to our core beliefs about others, the world and ourselves. After entering the Drama Triangle we can move between the different roles. Sometimes we tend to take on a specific role within a specific relationship or situation. At other times we shift roles within one conversation. The move from one role to another can happen very quickly and we can even move back and forth between roles in a matter of minutes.

> *'The Victim is not really as helpless as he feels, the Rescuer is not really helping and the Persecutor does not really have a valid complaint.'*
> — **CLAUDE STEINER**

A way out

No one in the Drama Triangle wins; it is a lose–lose situation, but there *is* a way out of this negative red-brain triangle of conflict. Disagreements, conflicts of interest and arguments are part of life. You are not able to control all of your circumstances or other people's behaviours but you can control your own brain state, even when you are in a conflict or disagreement. When you keep your own brain in the green zone, the dynamics of the conflict will change drastically and you will have better outcomes.

Solution Triangle

The green-brain or mindful version of conflict is represented in the Solution Triangle. The Solution Triangle is a more helpful alternative to the Drama Triangle and is based on the 'Winner's Triangle' proposed by Acey Choy in 1990.

Vulnerable
Awareness without judgment,
openness

Caring
Compassion, supporting
without taking over
responsibility

Assertive
Taking healthy
actions, setting
clear boundaries

VULNERABLE

Being vulnerable is the helpful version of being a victim. Vulnerability has two layers. First, it means being vulnerable and open towards yourself. Rather than suppressing thoughts and feelings, you mindfully allow them to be there even if they are not pretty or comfortable. One way of doing this is by using Acknowledge–Link–Let Go, the mindfulness tool for processing emotions (see page 59). When you are vulnerable and accept your emotions, instead of taking over, your feelings become like a compass that you can use to figure out what is being triggered for you and what need is not being met. This insight can then be used to figure out appropriate solutions and ways forward. The key combination to being vulnerable is accepting your thoughts and feelings without discounting your skills and abilities to problem solve.

For example, Jim's colleague fails to give him the information he needs to do his work. He feels frustrated and ignored and is in victim mode. He uses Acknowledge–Link–Let Go to process his feelings. When he thinks about the situation with a calm mind he sees that his colleague is not making his job hard on purpose. He is under a lot of pressure and is unable to handle his caseload. It is nothing personal.

The second layer of being vulnerable is sharing your thoughts and feelings with the person with whom you are in conflict, giving them insight into how you feel in a way that does not attack them or take over their responsibility. This position is called 'vulnerable' for a reason. Being vulnerable in conflict is not easy — it might feel uncomfortable or even unsafe — but it is very powerful.

A very effective way to give the other person insight into your thoughts and feelings is to use this technique:

'When you . . . It makes me feel/I feel . . .'

This approach helps you describe your experience of the situation in a way that is unlikely to raise resistance.

For example, Rachel's partner had been complaining all week about being tired and asked to postpone their date night because he did not have the energy to go out. Yet when his friends phoned him the following day and invited him to the football he accepted and stayed out until 2am. This left Rachel feeling angry and unloved. When she applied Acknowledge–Link–Let Go she tapped into the underlying hurt and sadness that was coming from a feeling of being rejected. Instead of feeling sorry for herself or giving her partner the silent treatment she chose to be vulnerable. She waited until the next day and told him:

'It really hurts me that you don't have the energy to go out with me but you can go out until 2am with your friends. It makes me feel rejected and as if you don't care about me.'

Her partner acknowledged that this was not fair and suggested he would take her out for dinner that evening.

ASSERTIVE

Being assertive is the green-brain version of being a persecutor. When you are assertive you are taking healthy actions that take care of your own unmet needs. You are not defending yourself but taking care of yourself. Assertiveness is something that follows from awareness and introspection. In order to understand what you really need, you first need to identify what you are really feeling underneath all the initial emotions of despair, anger or responsibility. Assertiveness begins with allowing yourself to pause and turn inwards. You can use Acknowledge–Link–Let Go for this and add to it the question: *How do I want to respond?*

Assertive actions are sometimes as simple as taking time for yourself because you realize you desperately need it, or saying no to requests because you need something else in that moment.

Following are some examples of what assertive actions can look like:
- Asking for what you want.
- Saying no to what you don't want.
- Giving feedback about behaviour that is causing a problem and being clear about what you would like to change.
- Negotiating solutions that work for everyone.
- Using your problem-solving skills to have your needs met, even when the other person does not change.

For example, Jamie's sister invited him to come over for dinner to spend time with his young nephew. Jamie had a full-on day at work and wasn't able to leave the office on time to beat the traffic, and he knew he had another stressful day ahead of him. He became frustrated that his sister always invited him at the last minute. He felt frustrated and stuck. When he applied Acknowledge–Link–Let Go he identified that most of his stress came from feeling that he was not given a choice. In his mind, he had to go. After breathing out and letting it go he asked himself the question: What do I need? He identified that he needed some down time. Then he asked himself the question: How do I want to respond? He decided to call his sister and explain his situation and his decision to stay home that evening. To his surprise she was very understanding and not bothered at all.

CARING

Being caring is the green-brain version of rescuing. Being caring means being compassionate without taking over responsibility or ignoring your own needs. A key skill in caring is listening without trying to 'fix things'.

Following are some examples of what caring actions can look like:
■ Invite others into problem-solving.
■ Be a mirror not a fixer; offer feedback on how you perceive the other person and their situation.
■ Give practical information that might help.

TIP: If you tend to adopt the rescuer role, this trick can help you to stay in the caring role: keep your back against the chair — because as soon as you enter the rescuer mode your posture will become active instead of relaxed.

For example, Martha was asked to volunteer for a charity. She valued the organization and felt honoured, yet she felt it was not the right time for her to take on this role. She was aware of her rescuing tendencies and chose to be assertive instead. She knew, however, how desperate the director was and she mirrored and linked this in their conversation. This made the director feel supported and heard even though Martha declined the offer. Martha then suggested several people the director could approach for the role.

When you find yourself in a conflict, pause and think about your role. Are you a victim, a persecutor or a rescuer? Once you have identified your position in the red-brain Drama Triangle, find the green-brain Solution Triangle version of your role and take the steps needed to move from your current role into the Solution Triangle role. This will change the dynamics of the situation and greatly increase the likelihood of a good outcome.

More techniques to help you be mindful in conflict

You can use mindfulness of the breath and mindfulness of the senses to help you back into the here and now and calm down. You can use Acknowledge–Link–Let Go to process the emotions you are feeling and come back to a green state. You can use self-inquiry to analyze the thoughts that are fuelling your red brain and turn them around to make your way back to the green zone.

But there are more techniques available. Here are some of my favourite techniques for being mindful in conflict.

1. THE BEGINNER'S MIND

In conflict, 'box thinking' can kick in. Applying the beginner's mind helps keep your brain in the green zone or brings it back to the green zone. Then, from this calmer and clearer place you can decide how you want to respond.

2. DOES IT REALLY MATTER?

It is often the small things — like a pair of socks left on the floor, the toothpaste cap off, a change of plans or an unanswered call — that become a reason for conflict. Sometimes we need to ask ourselves: Does it *really* matter? Taking a moment to consider the importance of things can help us stay in the green-brain zone and stop a way of thinking that will lead our brain into the red zone.

3. FOCUS ON INTENTION

One of the symptoms of the red brain is that we lose sight of the other person's intention because perspective-taking and empathy are blocked.

One way to keep your brain in the green zone — or bring it back — is to focus on the other person's intention. What is their intention? What are they trying to achieve? What is the goal or the need they are trying to fulfill?

4. WHOSE BUSINESS IS IT?

As soon as you interfere with someone else's business or responsibility you will feel stressed because you have no control. Their behaviour is not your responsibility, but theirs; how you *respond* to their behaviour is your responsibility.

When you stay in the part that actually *is* your responsibility, you are more likely to maintain a green-brain state, which makes you better at managing your response. As soon as you move into someone else's responsibility — *they should do this, they shouldn't think this, it's not fair for them to feel this* — you are moving towards the red zone. This leads to stress, making it harder to manage your behaviour.

How to tie it all together

You can use one technique at a time, but combining them can increase the effect. For example:

One client's biggest frustration was the fact that her partner left his shoes at the door rather than putting them on the rack. She had raised this with him many times, but it didn't change. This made her feel hurt and angry.

She applied Acknowledge–Link–Let Go. This made her see that his action — or inaction — made her feel as if he did not care about her or her needs and ultimately that he did not love her. She had given the pair of shoes the label 'I don't care what you think because I don't love you'. When you attach this label to a pair of shoes it becomes much more then just a pair of shoes. Every time she saw the shoes next to the door this label made her feel hurt and rejected.

Then we used the self-inquiry technique. This made her realize that the shoes left at the door did not actually mean that her partner did not love her, and that he showed in many ways that he did indeed love her. It also made her realize that her approach to the shoe situation was far from loving towards him.

Then she used the beginner's mind and as she looked at the facts she could see a pair of shoes in the hallway and herself becoming really angry.

She asked herself the question: Does it really matter that his shoes are next to the door instead of on the rack? The answer was no, it does not really matter.

She continued by asking: What is his intention? Her answer was that there probably was no negative intention. He didn't leave the shoes at the door with the intention of annoying her.

And finally she asked herself: Whose business is it? She saw that her partner putting his shoes next to the rack was *his* business. Her response to this was *her* business, her responsibility. She had been so caught up with her own thoughts and feelings about his business that she had failed to take care of hers. Because of that she had become angry, frustrated and her behaviour was far from loving and kind.

After this she decided that every time she saw his shoes next to the rack she would remind herself that it did *not* matter and use a mantra that reminded her that her partner loved her.

All of these strategies are tools for your mindfulness-in-conflict tool kit. They are all slightly different ways to reach the same end goal: to keep your brain in the green zone or help bring you back to the green zone. Some tools may work for you, some may not — the only way to find out is to try them a couple of times. Then you will naturally stick with the ones that work best for you.

 On-the-run tip: *Try to catch irritations and frustration early on and apply the techniques when things don't feel like a big deal yet. Prevention of conflict is better than cure.*

Chapter 13:
MINDFULNESS AND SELF-COMPASSION

One of the most profound skills that mindfulness practice has taught me is self-compassion. I have never before felt so comfortable with being kind and considerate towards myself. Historically when I entered the red or orange brain, my inner critic always showed up with a loud voice. Calming it down, making room for a more positive and supportive voice, felt very counter-intuitive, as if I were letting myself off the hook and would turn into a lazy, unproductive, irresponsible person.

My inner critic is not very nice. It is harsh, judgmental, angry, always doubting my abilities, mean and destructive. My inner critic would say things like:

- What's wrong with you? You idiot! Why can't you just get it right?
- You are such an impatient and horrible mother.
- Your nose is too big, you are too skinny and you definitely can't pull off wearing that dress.
- You have to work harder and get this done.
- They won't help you or back you up.

To put it simply, my inner critic is an arsehole.

I would never, ever talk to anyone else this way, yet I felt totally okay and comfortable talking to myself that way every single day. Before I started to practise mindfulness I never questioned this inner voice, instead I just accepted its chatter in my mind. Letting go of it felt surprisingly scary and unsafe, like I was forfeiting control, as if I were letting myself loose in a candy shop to eat all the candy without paying for it.

Most of us are able to identify with having an inner critic, and know it usually shows up when we are in the red zone. But why does it even exist? There is not one answer to this question; instead there are several contributors.

Childhood experiences

Childhood experiences are never all bad or all good, but the negative ones seem to echo through in the voice of the inner critic. Often the things our inner critic says resemble correcting messages we received either implicitly or explicitly from our caregivers. It all starts with the way a young child's brain works: it always perceives what the caregivers say as true and accurate.

For example, when a stressed-out father yells at his four-year-old son and tells him he is 'a disgusting boy', the child's brain is unable to see that actually he is just a child and that his father is the one acting in a disgusting way. The child accepts and believes what he is told. If this pattern is repeated on a regular basis, it is likely that the developing inner critic starts to use similar phrases.

When a young child consistently hears the message *you are the oldest so you should be (more) responsible*, this can lead to an inner voice that reminds the person that they are responsible for other people's behaviour and happiness.

If the message was *you are not as smart as your sister*, the inner-voice criticism might focus on commenting on a lack of abilities and skills.

If the message was *boys don't cry*, the inner critic is likely to tell the person to keep vulnerable emotions under control with thoughts like *you can't be weak*.

Attachment

Attachment theory is a psychological model that was first described by psychologist, psychiatrist and psychoanalyst John

Bowlby. Attachment theory describes the relationship between two humans, although the term 'attachment' is most often used to describe the relationship between a child and their caregiver. Essentially it describes the ability of a person to develop basic trust in their caregiver and consequently in themselves and others.

There are three forms of attachment: secure attachment, insecure attachment and avoidant attachment.

Secure attachment develops when the caregiver is available and responsive to the child's needs. A child who is securely attached to a caregiver feels safe, accepted and free to explore and make mistakes, because they trust that their caregiver will be there for them in times of need. They have a safe base to return to when things go wrong.

Insecure attachment (or ambivalent attachment) will develop when the caregiver is unpredictably or conditionally responsive to the child's needs. A child who is insecurely attached is more likely to feel angry, anxious or ambivalent in relationships and will have a tendency to both seek and resist contact.

Avoidant attachment develops when the caregiver consistently does not respond to the needs of the child. A child with avoidant attachment avoids disappointment and upset by no longer seeking closeness. They stay close enough to the parent to maintain protection but distant enough to avoid rejection. They will have strong underlying emotions such as sadness, anger and fear.

The nature of your relationship with your primary caregiver shapes the way you relate to yourself. You can experience secure attachment to yourself, insecure attachment and even avoidant attachment.

Someone with a secure attachment style is likely to feel capable, confident and able to relate to themselves in a kind and supportive way. They trust themselves and have a safe internal world. Their core beliefs will be along the lines of:

- I am okay as I am.
- I can cope.
- The world is safe to explore.
- I am supported.

Someone with an insecure attachment style is likely to only conditionally accept themselves, in a way that resembles the messages they received from their caregiver. For example:

- I am okay as long as I work hard/take care of others/am found attractive/others are happy.
- I have to . . .
- The world is safe as long as I . . .
- I am supported as long as I . . .

Someone with an avoidant attachment style is likely to be judgmental, harsh and unsupportive towards themselves. Their underlying core beliefs are likely to be something along these lines:

■ I am not okay.
■ I have to protect myself.
■ The world is not safe.
■ I am alone.

INSIGHT INSPIRATION

Is your self-talk mostly negative, neutral or positive?

1. Write down some of your negative self-talk. (This can be confronting and you might feel inclined to skip this step, but it is very helpful to know your negative self-talk so you can effectively change it.)

2. Given your past experiences, why does it make perfect sense that you would have these thoughts about yourself? ('Because they are true' is not the right answer!)

Mindfulness and the social brain

We all have attachment experiences and styles that have shaped the social structures of our brain and therefore shape how we feel about others, the world and ourselves. Studies show that mindfulness practice activates and reshapes these social structures. Because of neuroplasticity, practising mindfulness on a regular basis leads to stronger social circuits in the brain that become more easily activated. You could say that practising mindfulness on a regular basis reshapes the social structures in your brain into a more secure attachment structure.

As Daniel Siegel puts it:

> 'Mindfulness is not only a form of attention training and it is not only a form of affect regulation training. Mindfulness is a relational process where you become your own best friend.'

How to grow a kinder inner voice

Mindfulness practice softens old constructs that dictate how we see and relate to ourselves. This process opens up the way for developing a kinder inner voice. When thoughts like *'you idiot'*, *'you are never going to succeed'* or *'no one really cares about you'* come up, there are various techniques you can use.

1. STOP RESPONDING

One way of approaching a self-critical thought is by noticing it without engaging with it or responding to it; a thought is just a thought unless you believe it and engage with it. Then gently and kindly turn your attention back to your breath, your senses or whatever it is that you are doing. This way you don't give the thought any power or control. In time the unhelpful thought will come up less and less because you are not reinforcing it.

2. BEFRIEND THE INNER CRITIC

One way to calm your critical inner voice is by actually 'befriending' it. Try to be curious about what is triggering it without believing everything it says. This helps the healthy adult part of you to stay in control while you find out what underlying hurt is triggered so you can address that. You can apply the ALL technique (see page 59) for this.

> *'Angry is just sad's bodyguard.'*
> **— LIZA PALMER**

3. MANTRA

When you practise a kind and supportive mantra regularly, you will be surprised at how quickly your inner voice becomes kinder. You can use the helpful, green-brain thoughts that come up when you go through the ALL process and turn them into a mantra for that period, or you can use the affirmations discussed in Chapter

7. It does not matter what you use as long as the thoughts are positive and kind and you practise them on a regular basis.

Back yourself up, instead of beating yourself up

Learning to back yourself up with kind, compassionate self-talk, instead of beating yourself up with harsh and critical self-talk, will eliminate one of your most powerful red-brain triggers and drastically increase green-brain activity.

My mean, self-critical voice still shows up every now and then. When it does I can see it for what it is and gently and kindly turn my focus back to thoughts that are actually helpful to me in that moment. When the feeling that I constantly need to learn, grow and achieve more all the time creeps back in — you might call it perfectionism — I remind myself that a state of being present and content with where I am at will be more effective in reaching my goals. To remind me of this, I have a mantra sitting on my desk that says: *You are exactly where you need to be.*

The underlying truth is that I am okay just as I am in this moment. Every time I read this mantra I am reminded of this truth and it calms my rushing tendencies and activates my green brain. Then in that green-brain state I am much more effective and efficient in working towards my goals in a sustainable and fun way.

On-the-run tip: *For a quick boost in self-compassion, place one hand on your chest and one hand on your stomach. This resembles giving yourself an encouraging hug. Your brain will respond by activating the social engagement system and releasing oxytocin.*

CONCLUDING THOUGHTS

I hope you have enjoyed this book, but most of all I hope that it has helped you realize the value of cultivating your green brain.

There is a mismatch between what science knows and what most people do. Here is what science knows:

- Stress is unhelpful, toxic to our minds and our bodies. It creates conflict and reduces success.
- Retraining your brain to reduce stress is free and can be done any time and anywhere.
- The secret to a happy and successful life is not just hard work or circumstance; it is being in control of your brain by being in control of your thoughts.

Here is the best part, and we all intuitively know this already: you simply can't drive yourself to exhaustion and at the same time perform well and feel good.

So, if you repair the mismatch between what science knows and what you practise in your everyday life, if you apply science to taking care of your brain, if you get past the productivity myth, then you can renew your mind and renew your life.

Let me leave you with this story:

An old Cherokee told his grandson:

'There is a battle between two wolves inside us all. One is evil. It is anger, jealousy, greed, resentment, inferiority, lies and ego. The other is good. It is joy, peace, love, hope, humility, kindness, empathy and truth.'

The boy thought about it and asked, 'Grandfather, which wolf wins?'

The old man quietly replied, 'The one you feed.'

— Unknown

REFERENCES

CHAPTER 2

Kathryn Birnie, Michael Speca and Linda E. Carlson, 'Exploring self-compassion and empathy in the context of mindfulness-based stress reduction (MBSR)', *Stress and Health*, December 2010.

Sarah Bowen, Katie Witkiewitz, Tiara M. Dillworth, Neharika Chawla, Tracy L. Simpson, Brian D. Ostafin, Mary E. Larimer, Arthur W. Blume, George A. Parks and G. Alan Marlatt, 'Mindfulness meditation and substance use in an incarcerated population', *Psychology of Addictive Behaviors*, September 2006.

Richard J. Davidson, Jon Kabat-Zinn, Jessica Schumacher, Melissa Rosenkranz, Daniel Muller, Saki F. Santorelli, Ferris Urbanowski, Anne Harrington, Katherine Bonus and John F. Sheridan, 'Alterations in brain and immune function produced by mindfulness meditation', *Psychosomatic Medicine*, July 2003.

Ian Donald, Paul Taylor, Sheena Johnson, Cary Cooper, Susan Cartwright and Susannah Robertson, 'Work environments, stress, and productivity: An examination using ASSET', *International Journal of Stress Management*, November 2005.

Norman A.S. Farb, Adam K. Anderson and Zindel V. Segal, 'The mindful brain and emotion regulation in mood disorders', *Canadian Journal of Psychiatry*, February 2012.

Paul Grossman, Ludger Niemann, Stefan Schmidt, Harald Walach, 'Mindfulness-based stress reduction and health benefits: A meta-analysis', *Journal of Psychosomatic Research*, July 2004.

Stefan G. Hofmann, Alice T. Sawyer, Ashley A. Witt and Diana Oh, 'The effect of mindfulness-based therapy on anxiety and depression: A meta-analytic review', *Journal of Consulting and Clinical Psychology*, April 2010.

Phan Y. Hong, David A. Lishner, Kim H. Han, Elizabeth A. Huss, 'The positive impact of mindful eating on expectations of food liking', *Mindfulness*, June 2011.

J.W. Hughes, D.M. Fresco, R. Myerscough, M.H. van Dulmen, L.E. Carlson and R. Josephson, 'Randomized controlled trial of mindfulness-based stress reduction for prehypertension', *Psychosomatic Medicine*, October 2013.

Ute R. Hülsheger, Hugo J.E. M Alberts, Alina Feinholdt and Jonas W.B. Lang, 'Benefits of mindfulness at work: The role of mindfulness in emotion regulation, emotional exhaustion, and job satisfaction', *Journal of Applied Psychology*, March 2013.

Itai Ivtzan, Hanna E. Gardner and Zhanar Smailova, 'Mindfulness meditation and curiosity: The contributing factors to wellbeing and the process of closing the self-discrepancy gap', *International Journal of Wellbeing*, 2011.

Shamini Jain, Shauna L. Shapiro, Summer Swanick, Scott C. Roesch, Paul J. Mills, Iris Bell and Gary E.R. Schwartz, 'A randomized controlled trial of mindfulness meditation versus relaxation training: Effects on distress, positive states of mind, rumination, and distraction', *Annals of Behavioral Medicine*, February 2007.

Muhammad Jamal, 'Job stress and job performance controversy: An empirical assessment', *Organizational Behavior and Human Performance*, February 1984.

Shian-Ling Keng, Moria J. Smoski and Clive J. Robins, 'Effects of mindfulness on psychological health: A review of empirical studies', *Clinical Psychology Review*, August 2011.

Cara Murphy and James MacKillop, 'Living in the here and now: Interrelationships between impulsivity, mindfulness, and alcohol misuse', *Psychopharmacology*, January 2012.

Esther K. Papies, Lawrence W. Barsalou and Ruud Custers, 'Mindful attention prevents mindless impulses', *Social Psychological and Personality* Science, May 2012.

Shauna L. Shapiro, Gary E. Schwartz and Ginny Bonner, 'Effects of mindfulness-based stress reduction on medical and premedical students', *Journal of Behavioral Medicine*, December 1998.

Bruce W. Smith, Alexis J. Ortiz, Laurie E. Steffen, Erin M. Tooley, Kathryn T. Wiggins, Elizabeth A. Yeater, John D. Montoya and Michael L. Bernard, 'Mindfulness is associated with fewer PTSD symptoms, depressive symptoms, physical symptoms, and alcohol problems in urban firefighters', *Journal of Consulting and Clinical Psychology*, October 2011.

Mark A. Runco, *Creativity: Theories and Themes: Research, Development, and Practice*, Elsevier, 2014.

J.M.G. Williams, Y. Alatiq, C. Crane, T. Barnhofer, M.J.V. Fennell, D.S. Duggan, S. Hepburn and G.M. Goodwin, 'Mindfulness-based Cognitive Therapy (MBCT) in bipolar disorder: Preliminary evaluation of immediate effects on between-episode functioning', *Journal of Affective Disorders*, April 2008.

CHAPTER 3

Stephen W. Porges, 'The polyvagal theory: Phylogenetic substrates of a social nervous system', *International Journal of Psychophysiology*, October 2001.

CHAPTER 5

Abiola Keller, Kristin Litzelman, Lauren E. Wisk, Torsheika Maddox, Erika Rose Cheng, Paul D. Creswell and Whitney P. Witt, 'Does the perception that stress affects health matter? The association with health and mortality', *Health Psychology*, September 2012.

J.P. Jamieson, M.K. Nock and W.B. Mendes, 'Mind over matter: Reappraising arousal improves cardiovascular and cognitive responses to stress', *Journal of Experimental Psychology: General*, August 2012.

CHAPTER 7

Barbara L. Fredrickson, 'The broaden–and–build theory of positive emotions', *Philosophical Transactions of the Royal Society B: Biological Sciences*, September 2004.

CHAPTER 8

Sian L. Beilock and Rob Gray, 'From attentional control to attentional spillover: A skill-level investigation of attention, movement, and performance outcomes', *Human Movement Science*, December 2012.

Amy J.C. Cuddy, Caroline A. Wilmuth and Dana R. Carney, 'The benefit of power posing before a high-stakes social evaluation', Harvard Business School Working Paper, September 2012.

Susan Goldin-Meadow and Sian L. Beilock, 'Action's influence on thought: The case of gesture', *Perspectives on Psychological Science*, November 2010.

Carly Kontra, Susan Goldin-Meadow and Sian L. Beilock, 'Embodied learning across the life span', *Topics in Cognitive Science*, October 2012.

M.A. Wollmer, C. de Boer, N. Kalak, J. Beck, T. Götz, T. Schmidt, M. Hodzic, U. Bayer, T. Kollman, K. Kollewe, D. Sonmez, K. Duntsch, M.D. Haug, M. Schedlowski, M. Hatzinger, D. Dressler, S. Brand, E. Holsboer-Trachsler and T.H. Kruger, 'Facing depression with botulinum toxin: A randomized controlled trial', *Journal of Psychiatric Research*, May 2012.

CHAPTER 9

Bruno S. Frey and Alois Stutzer, 'Happiness research: State and prospects', *Review of Social Economy*, June 2005.

Richard M. Ryan and Edward L. Deci, 'On happiness and human potentials: A review of research on hedonic and eudaimonic well-being', *Annual Review of Psychology*, February 2001.

CHAPTER 10

Richard Wiseman, *The Luck Factor*, Random House, 2011.

CHAPTER 11

Sara B. Algoe and Baldwin Way, 'Evidence for a role of the oxytocin system, indexed by genetic variation in CD38, in the social bonding effects of expressed gratitude', *Social Cognitive and Affective Neuroscience*, January 2014.

Michael Babyak, James A. Blumenthal, Steve Herman, Parinda Khatri, Murali Doraiswamy, Kathleen Moore, Edward Craighead, Tei T. Baldewicz and Krishnan K. Ranga, 'Exercise treatment for major depression: Maintenance of therapeutic benefit at 10 months', *Psychosomatic Medicine*, September/October 2000.

Margaret M. Bass, Catherine A. Duchowny, Maria M. Llabre, 'The effect of therapeutic horseback riding on social functioning in children with autism', *Journal of Autism and Developmental Disorders*, September 2009.

Marian R. Banks and William A. Banks, 'The effects of animal-assisted therapy on loneliness in an elderly population in long-term care facilities, *The Journals of Gerontology: Series A*, December 2001.

Andrea Beetz, Kerstin Uvnäs-Moberg, Henri Julius and Kurt Kotrschal, 'Psychosocial and psychophysiological effects of human–animal interactions: The possible role of oxytocin', *Frontiers in Psychology*, 2012.

Adam J. Guastella, Philip B. Mitchell and Mark R. Dadds, 'Oxytocin increases gaze to the eye region of human faces', *Biological Psychiatry*, January 2008.

Kristiann C. Heesch, Yolanda R. van Gellecum, Nicola W. Burton, Jannique G.Z. van Uffelen and Wendy J. Brown, 'Physical activity, walking, and quality of life in women with depressive symptoms', *American Journal of Preventive Medicine*, January 2015.

J. Holt-Lunstad, T.B. Smith and J.B. Layton, 'Social relationships and mortality risk: A meta-analytic review', *PLOS Medicine*, July 2010.

Michael W. Kraus, Cassy Huang and Dacher Keltner, 'Tactile communication, cooperation, and performance: An ethological study of the NBA', *EMOTION*, October 2010.

Egil W. Martinsen, A. Medhus and L. Sandvik, 'Effects of aerobic exercise on depression: A controlled study', *British Medical Journal*, July 1985.

Murray B. Stein, 'Sweating away the blues: Can exercise treat depression?', *American Journal of Preventive Medicine*, January 2005.

Kevin Wheldall, Kate Bevan and Kath Shortall, 'A touch of reinforcement: The effects of contingent teacher touch on the classroom behaviour of young children', *Educational Review*, 1986.

P.J. Zak, A.A. Stanton and S. Ahmadi, 'Oxytocin increases generosity in humans', *PLOS ONE*, November 2007.

CHAPTER 13

Karen Goodall, Anna Trejnowska and Stephen Darling, 'The relationship between dispositional mindfulness, attachment security and emotion regulation', *Personality and Individual Differences*, April 2012.

Daniel J. Siegel, 'Mindful awareness, mindsight, and neural integration, *The Humanistic Psychologist*, June 2009.

INDEX